Contagion and the Responsibility of Networks

'Contagion' is a crucial term in the theory of networks, that is nowadays employed to study increasingly diverse issues such as financial crises, epidemics, and fake news. It provides a unifying framework to describe various social and economic phenomena that occur within different networks — involving various forms of contagion.

This book discusses contagion over social and economic networks, and its consequences for modern societies. It starts with an accessible but solid introduction to basic concepts of the theory of networks, with intuitive explanations and examples both of networks that shape our daily lives, and of how researchers analyze them. It then focuses specifically on contagion, and on its importance for societies. Three crucial examples are analyzed more in depth: epidemiological contagion, fake news and financial crises. The conclusions show how various societal problems — each consequence of some form of contagion — call for similar policy measures: a pre-emptive and comprehensive effort in collecting the required information, and a shift in the concept of individual responsibility itself.

This is a book for any reader who is interested in how contagion and networks shape modern society.

Pietro Battiston is an Assistant Professor in Economics at University of Pisa, Italy.

Contagion and the Responsibility of Networks

From Pandemics to Financial Crises and Fake News

Pietro Battiston

Routledge
Taylor & Francis Group
LONDON AND NEW YORK

First published 2025
by Routledge
4 Park Square, Milton Park, Abingdon, Oxon, OX14 4RN

and by Routledge
605 Third Avenue, New York, NY 10158

Routledge is an imprint of the Taylor & Francis Group, an informa business

British Library Cataloguing-in-Publication Data
A catalogue record for this book is available from the British Library

ISBN: 9781032791975 (hbk)
ISBN: 9781032791982 (pbk)
ISBN: 9781003490951 (ebk)

DOI: 10.4324/9781003490951

Typeset in Times New Roman
by Newgen Publishing UK

Contents

List of figures *vi*
About the author *viii*
Preface *ix*
Acknowledgments *xiii*

1 What are networks? 1

2 Externalities and contagion 24

3 Epidemics and networks 39

4 Information diffusion as contagion 67

5 Epidemics in finance 90

6 Network responsibility 119

Image credits *133*
Index *135*

Figures

1.1 Graphic representations of example networks 3
1.2 Directed/Undirected network 5
1.3 (a): X followers; (b): Facebook friends 5
1.4 Weighted/Unweighted network 6
1.5 External measure of importance 8
1.6 Spatial/Non-spatial network 9
1.7 Possible growth modes of a network 9
1.8 A network of three X users 11
1.9 A map of the area around Lake Michigan 14
1.10 Basic network structures 16
1.11 Two very different web pages with the same indegree 18
1.12 The random surfer 19
2.1 Global and local externalities 27
2.2 The diffusion of a hypothetical messaging app 28
2.3 The social network of 10 hypothetical Facebook profiles 29
2.4 Rewiring example, applied to the 'core' network from Figure 2.3 30
3.1 Map of the region from where the 2013 Ebola outbreak originated 41
3.2 Examples of fixed–degree networks 46
3.3 Growth of positive cases in the early phase of epidemics 48
3.4 Weighted network corresponding to Table 3.1 52
3.5 Incidence of COVID–19 by age group, USA, 2022 53
3.6 Incidence of measles by age group in the European Union during 2017 53
3.7 Contact matrices from the POLYMOD project 56
3.8 Connection intensities between fifteen age classes, from the POLYMOD project (average across countries) 57
3.9 Connection intensities between age classes in Zimbabwe 58
4.1 Number of views for the *Gangnam Style* video on YouTube 68
4.2 An example of a cascade over X 71
4.3 An example of a multiplex network made of six nodes connected over three different layers 72

4.4 The perceived and actual networks including the Passenger, the Colleague, the Seller, and myself 81
5.1 A simple network of credit 96
5.2 Bank A is connected to shipbuilding firms via two paths 97
5.3 Spread between Italian/Spanish treasury bills and German ones 99
5.4 Three tennis players 100
5.5 A loop in the credit network 101
5.6 Example of securitization 105
5.7 A bank lending to firms and to individuals 108
5.8 Breaking the tennis players' cycle 112
6.1 Value of the STOXX Europe 600 Automobiles & Parts Index in 2008 121
6.2 Example of cross–ownership network 122
6.3 Panel located at the boundary between the drainage basins of Danube and Rhein 129

About the author

Pietro Battiston is an Assistant Professor in Economics at the University of Pisa, Italy. After a degree in Mathematics, he obtained an MSc in Economics from the University of Bologna and a PhD in Economics from the University of Milan Bicocca. His main research interests are Network Theory, Experimental Economics, Tax Compliance, and Bibliometrics. He has published in prestigious international journals including the *Scandinavian Journal of Economics, Health Policy, World Development, Games and Economic Behavior*. He is active in the popularization of economics via articles on general media, talks in festivals, and in online videos. His website is https://pietrobattiston.it.

Preface

In 2007 and 2008, a global financial crisis sent shockwaves through the world's economies, bringing to ruin even large and established financial institutions like Lehman Brothers; today it is considered by many to be the worst financial crisis since the Great Depression of the 1930s. Between 2014 and 2016, the Western African Ebola virus epidemic wreaked havoc primarily in Guinea, Liberia, and Sierra Leone, ultimately taking more than eleven thousand lives and earning the designation as the most widespread outbreak of the Ebola virus in history, only to be completely eclipsed, a few years later, by the COVID–19 pandemic. Starting from the 2016 US presidential elections, the spread of misinformation and fake news across the Internet has increasingly characterized the path to voting beginning with fake Twitter accounts run by Russian bots and spilling over into mainstream media coverage, making the ability to discern fact from fiction nearly impossible, even to the trained skeptic. While these three global catastrophic events may seem disparate, a closer examination reveals they share a surprising number of commonalities. Firstly, they represent important problems for society. Despite (or because of?) the fact that some people were able to profit from them, it is easy to agree that in general, humanity would have been better off had the stock market not crashed, had COVID–19 not spread, had information sources always been trustworthy. If society could find a way to prevent similar crises in the future, such measures should certainly be taken. Secondly, these events made certain people suffer the consequences of others' decisions, or actions. And in many cases — this is where things become more interesting — such decisions were made in good faith, without the intention to cause harm. These instances of involuntary harm (or, seldomly, good) are central to this book, as they play a fundamental role in our daily lives because of how our modern society is structured. Thirdly — and here comes the good news — we can better understand these crises, and how to limit their harmful consequences in the future, by increasing our knowledge of networks. That a single concept or tool — networks — can help society tackle such diverse issues might seem a very bold claim. But the truth is that networks are in fact being used to do much more than this. The first chapter of this book presents a large number of applications of the theory of networks, but even so, there are many more that are not included because they are outside the scope of a single book. Trained as a mathematician but soon converted to economics, my interest in networks, which I have now been researching for almost fifteen years, originated from economic — certainly not epidemiological — applications. But this book stems from more than mere speculating on the applicability of my everyday tools to new disciplines. It slowly took form, in my mind and in discussions with colleagues, as I found out that scholars such as computer scientists, physicists, ecologists, sociologists, epidemiologists and many others were already working every day with ideas and tools similar to those I was using. In their research, I could find 'nodes', 'edges', 'centrality', 'loops', 'clustering', and other related concepts, which will be presented in Chapter 1 and which form the building blocks of the theory of networks — and not only economic networks. When comparing my research with theirs, it was clear that the similarities in the terminology we used were just the tip of the iceberg: we were really posing similar questions, and sometimes finding similar answers, though applied to completely different data, and phenomena. And not by chance: the diffusion of methods and concepts throughout different disciplines has been at least as important, for the success of social networks analysis, as the theoretical development of such methods and concepts. One of the wonderful aspects of academia is that scholars can generally decide what to research. Consequently, it is not surprising that researchers are often passioned about discussing their research. However, my urge to write this book had more to do with my citizen self than with my researcher self. The more I discovered that seemingly unrelated problems and phenomena, characterizing modern societies, had similar explanations, and cures, the more urgency I felt to share with friends and colleagues, oftentimes studying issues where underlying networks play a central, but hidden, role, this new view of the world. Importantly, this awareness is also within reach of citizens, and policy makers, because the concepts discussed in the following pages correspond to intuitions that we often form spontaneously while observing the world around us. Network theory enhances these intuitions and our understanding of phenomena such as epidemics and crises in two main ways. Firstly, it allows us to reconnect them to unifying explanations — to see the common motive behind them — and secondly, it allows us to substantiate them with hard evidence, removing them from the realm of guesswork. Indeed, the possibility of basing the analysis of economic and social networks on data from a multitude of sources is what has really enabled this approach to make huge leaps forward in recent decades. The mathematics employed in the theory of networks is beautiful, and effective, and has undergone intriguing developments in the new millennium. But in the end, most of this mathematics is not particularly new. What is new, and what makes network theory far more popular today than it was just twenty years ago, is the increase in the amount of network data available to researchers, policy makers, and citizens in general. In part, this increase in available data is a natural consequence of the evolution of information technology. One could argue, for instance, that taking the subway today in London is not very different from taking the same subway forty years ago. But below the surface, there is a significant difference in that today's electronic tickets allow the transport authority to reconstruct, store, and analyze riders' journeys inside the subway network, and to use such data to plan further improvements to the system. So in this case, a system that mechanically works more or less the same as it did in 1980 now produces large amounts of data, which becomes an integrated asset in the transport authority's toolbox. In other cases, network data is the result of brand new phenomena that just did not exist before. What were the Facebook, TikTok, or World Wide Web, of the 1980s? Certainly one can draw parallels with phone calls, paper mail, and newspaper articles, but these would be at best faint metaphors for today's disruptive communication technologies. And virtually all new communication technologies happen to produce large amounts of network data, which communication platforms yearn for to even more effectively profile and attract customers. That data exists does not mean that everyone has access to it — luckily so, in the case of some networks, such as communication networks. Privacy, on one hand, and transparency, on the other, will be recurring themes, particularly in the last chapter, and there is no obvious rule about who should have access to certain data. In general, however, it is ironic that governments — who are responsible for many of the infrastructures and institutions our societies rely on — have much less access to data about their citizens than some private firms do, and researchers typically even less so. When considering certain important networks that transcend national borders, this can become a fundamental issue because no single government or firm can gain access to a description — even a simplified one — of the entire network. True, much of this book's focus is on the unintentional involuntary effects that the actions and choices of individuals can have on others through social networks. But there will be room to discuss malicious behavior within these networks, and to examine how this behavior can feed on a lack of awareness from other members in the network and create pockets of illegality that represent a hazard to the entire system. Parts of networks that are hidden from regulators are akin to city neighborhoods that are inaccessible to law enforcement: they easily become a hive of problematic behavior that contaminates other neighborhoods. And this is what happens every day inside global networks which are crucial for our lives. Indeed, networks such as financial and communication networks are not planned and created by state authorities; rather, they form spontaneously from the interaction of millions of individual participants — and this is what makes them so powerful, and essential. But like a city that grows spontaneously, they require regulation to quickly adapt and grow responsibly and efficiently, which is a very difficult task when networks are international in nature, and no single national authority is able to gain a complete view of the network members and all their interactions — let alone regulate them. Furthermore, regulation becomes incredibly difficult when parts of the network do their best to hide from regulators, while simultaneously remaining attached to, and benefiting from the network itself, like sophisticated leeches. One essential takeaway from this book is that, before even thinking about which rules to impose on the growth and behavior of social networks, we must be able to 'map' them, just like we map cities. Researchers and policy makers must pro-actively study the links, and the flows over them, that shape the lives of today and tomorrow, rather than reacting, often tardily, by closing the stable door after the horse has bolted. The level of government intervention in economic and social issues is often considered to be the result of a push and pull between the opposite extremes of state planning, which squeezes individual freedoms, and stateless liberalism, which does nothing to protect said freedoms. But new developments in social sciences call for a change in direction, focusing on evidence-based policies that adapt in a flexible, yet accountable, way to the changing needs of society. However such evidence — the kind of evidence required to understand and regulate complex systems — does not necessarily reveal itself spontaneously. The ability of governments and researchers to aggregate and analyze the complex behavior of our societies, and to provide timely diagnoses, already represents a powerful antidote to panic crises, which are a constant risk in the modern world. The importance of this ability to curb and control panic is only going to grow over time, as we become increasingly interconnected and dependent on our neighbors. This is the time in which the very concept of 'neighbor' can be extended widely, to the point of occasionally including individuals closely related to us despite living thousands of kilometers away. This is the time in which becoming involved in discussions, partnerships, and deals with people on the other side of the globe has suddenly become as easy as tapping on a screen — or having someone else tap for us, sometimes without us even knowing it. Hence, this is the time in which we must adopt a systematic approach to the analysis of how money, risk, news, and viruses can propagate on the social and economic networks that surround us, for these networks and connections have never been as pervasive in our daily lives as they are right now and will be going forward. This book exposes the chains of events by which phenomena such as epidemics, financial crises and fake news threaten our existence as human beings. The answer is not simple, but neither is it necessarily complicated. It is somewhat complex — a complexity that we must learn to understand and tame, if we want to protect our society. In fact, while the first chapter of this book provides many answers, the others leave a range of open questions. The answers, despite being simple, can help us gain an understanding of many phenomena in our modern societies; and as for the open questions, despite the difficulties in solving them, we simply cannot afford to neglect them.

Acknowledgments

This book is the result of a chain of wonderful people linked by a sequence of fortunate events: I am deeply indebted to each of them. To Luca Stanca, for being such a great PhD advisor, and for first directing me toward the study of networks; to Sharon Harrison, for her desire to break the barriers between research fields, and for her invitation to present the core ideas of this book at Columbia University in February 2017; to Bridget Flannery O'Connor, for her unwavering belief that these network ideas that researchers were discussing were worth conveying to the larger public; to my coauthor and friend Elena Sedano Varo, for the enthusiasm she has shown since the first time we discussed the book, and for all the discussions that followed; to Jessica Newman, for being so professional and at the same time so involved in the project; to Monica Albertoni and Paola Pecchioli for their professionalism and helpfulness; to Andy Humphries, for believing in this project since the beginning, and for Yarisa Wahlang Kharbuli for guiding me to the finish line. I would like to thank Alessia Melegaro for her enlightening suggestions on the world of epidemiological networks, three anonymous reviewers for their stimulating and thought-provoking comments, and all those who helped me shape the book with their insightful comments and suggestions: Tom Alterman, Stefano Battiston, Marco D'Errico, Simona Gamba, Alessandro Parise, Michele Romano, Valentina Rotondi, Alessandro Santoro ... and those whose name I cannot disclose. I would also like to thank my family, who did much more than just provide moral support, Elisa, the best possible traveling companion in this journey and in the ones to come, and Arianna and Agnese, who joined along the way, gifting me with a tangible image of what the future looks like.

1 What are networks?

When John Paul Young first sang his hit 'Love is in the air', he did not want us to imagine that a portion of the nitrogen and oxygen molecules in the air had been suddenly *replaced* with microparticles of love, scattered throughout all the Earth's atmosphere. He was rather describing a new way of *looking* at, *listening* at, and *experiencing* the world around him.

The theory of networks — while not quite as sentimental — can be viewed in a similar fashion, as a new way of looking at the world we see every day. A way so useful and pervasive as to lead some researchers to claim that 'networks are everywhere'. Again, this is not like affirming the presence of some mysterious substance you cannot see. It is more like saying that there is something you *do* see every day, but you do not necessarily recognize.

When observing the world around us, we generally do not perceive the things we see as collections of atoms or atomic reactions. Instead we see trees, plants, water, food, sometimes even air. In fact, a person can still experience the burning of wood, the growth of a plant, the evaporation of water, and the overcooking of food, even if he has lived his entire life without knowing what an atom is. However, if a person knows what an atom is and understands how atoms interact with one another, then he is able to explain why wood burns, how plants grow, how water evaporates, and why food overcooks. Networks also play pivotal roles in most aspects of our daily lives, although we may not recognize them unless we look closely.

Still, one might object, some advanced microscopes are able to observe individual atoms, so they are not *just* a matter of 'interpretation'. Where are the microscopes to examine networks?

Indeed, some networks can be studied by looking in a microscope. But most often, studying a network requires the opposite effort — to zoom out, broaden the view, and see multiple pieces as part of the same structure. Only when we consider many banks as part of a connected financial system, many individuals as part of a connected society, and many firms as part of a connected market, does the unifying picture begin to take shape. From this vantage point, the theory of networks provides a simple and general way to store — in a computer, for instance — many aspects and features of reality around us, and to

DOI: 10.4324/9781003490951-1

examine both the workings of entire systems and of specific parts. The utility of networks, however, extends beyond new ways of representing or describing the world. Networks are also useful instruments for *improving* several aspects of our society, in ways that would hardly be conceivable otherwise. In the next chapter, several examples will be provided of how network concepts can help fight epidemics, fake news, and financial crises.

Like any scientific theory, the theory of networks is simply a collection of concepts, methods, and results: even the most advanced theory ever proposed only explains *some* phenomena and not others. But despite the theory of networks being extremely powerful, its basic ingredients are in fact quite elementary and, consequently, quite general. The theory is so general, in fact, that many contexts naturally fit with many *different* network interpretations (a bit like if, when John Paul Young was writing his song, the air, the trees and the sea were reminding him more than just *one* girl). Given the simplicity and general nature of the theory, it has been successfully employed by researchers in a variety of disciplines such as physics, economics, mathematics, biology, medicine, computer science, among others.

1.1 Fundamental concepts

Two main ingredients are required to discuss a 'network': a collection of *things*, and a collection of *connections* among such things. These purposely vague terms reflect the fact that 'things' can be anything, from atoms to banks, from sharks to words, and 'connections' can also vary widely in form. That being said, in the theory of networks, the things to connect are typically called 'nodes', and the connections between nodes are called 'edges' (or 'links'). So all a network requires is a set of things with some connection to each other, that is, a set of nodes and a set of edges between such nodes.

The networks depicted vary widely in size and in the kind of relationship analyzed, but they can all be reduced to the two basic ingredients. We see some familiar networks, such as the *online social networks* Facebook (Figure 1.1a) and X, formerly known as Twitter (Figure 1.1b), and some that are likely less familiar, such as the social relations inside a community of *sharks* (Figure 1.1c), which has allowed researchers to identify how much time specific sharks were spending with other sharks within the same social network.[1] Some networks, such as that of logic variables (Figure 1.1d) taken from the computer science literature, can be very abstract; others, such as the network of international trade between industrial sectors (Figure 1.1e), describe the actual movement of tons of goods. Networks can be comprised of just a few nodes, like the communication structure from an economic experiment in Figure 1.1f,[2] or billions of nodes, like the Facebook network in Figure 1.1a.

The examples in Figure 1.1 look different compared to each other, but they are still much more similar than one might expect: ultimately, all are composed of dots and lines connecting those dots. Moreover, they can be *described* in a similar way and hence *recorded*, a bit like the alphabet allows us to write

	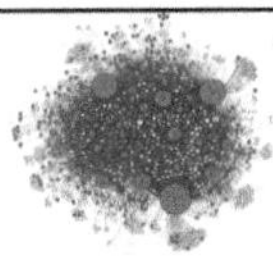 (a)	 (b)	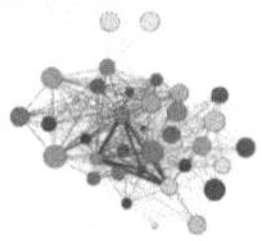 (c)	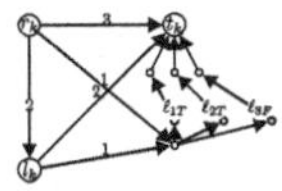 (d)
Nodes	Facebook accounts	X/Twitter accounts	sharks	logic variables
Edges	friendship	followers	hanging out	connectors
	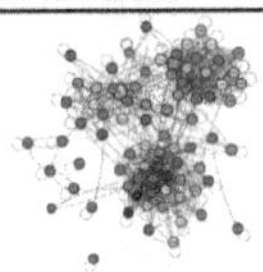 (e)	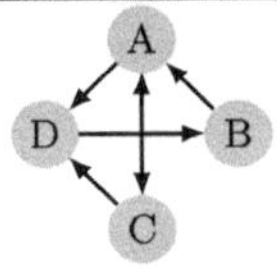 (f)	 (g)	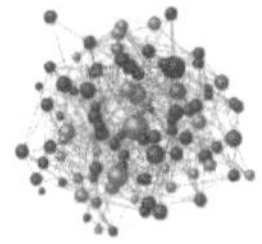 (h)
Nodes	industrial sectors	individuals	adolescents	banks
Edges	trade	communication	sexual relationships	loans
	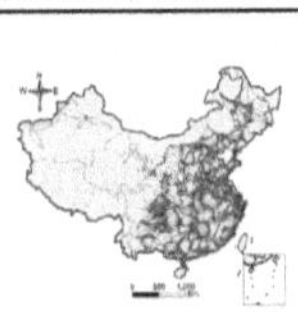 (i)	 (j)	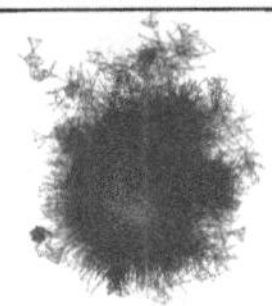 (k)	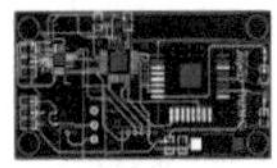 (l)
Nodes	municipalities	cities	actors	electronic components
Edges	migration	highways	collaboration	electric tracks
	 (m)	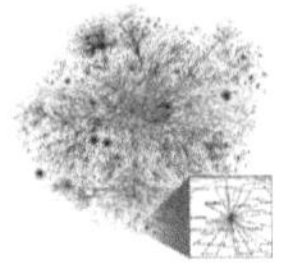 (n)	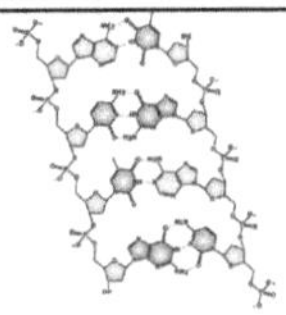 (o)	 (p)
Nodes	scientific articles	web pages	atoms	authors of scientific papers
Edges	citations	hyperlinks	chemical bonds	coauthorship

Figure 1.1 Graphic representations of example networks

both poems and shopping lists. Once we establish the network interpretation — that is, defining a node and defining an edge — then the network of social relations between sharks can be described in a form that makes it potentially indistinguishable from the network of international trade.

Some networks describe, like photographs, something that, at a given moment in time, *exists* and can be observed – be it something tangible, such as the road network, or something more abstract, such as the network of X accounts. Alternatively, in the network of sharks in Figure 1.1c and that of migration in Figure 1.1i, edges do not represent any object or concept, but rather measure the *intensity* or *frequency* of something that takes place over time. There is no physical, or digital, link between sharks or cities being described, just something that *happens*. Friendship on Facebook is a relationship of the first kind (it is, at a given moment in time, either present or absent). Friendship in a more 'real' sense is a relationship of the second kind, and it can, in principle, be measured by how often two people interact or how much time they spend communicating. Our network ingredients are general enough to describe both kind of relationships. There will even be cases in which we are interested in both an 'actual' network — take the roads network, for instance — *and* a network describing a behavior or phenomenon that takes place over the former — such as the number of cars passing on each road on a given day. In principle, this does not limit our attention to networks or behaviors for which *humans* are responsible: microbiologists have discovered that fungi cooperatively build huge underground networks connecting plants between them, and that these networks allow the flow of nutrients that is vital both to the fungi and to the plants.[3] But in practice, this book will mostly focus on social and economic networks, both for their relevance for our lives, and because they easily feature rich structures and intriguing phenomena.

Nodes and edges are the building blocks of the theory of networks, and in order to gain a better understanding of specific networks, we must be able to describe their foundations. While this is done in different ways throughout the different fields of the network literature, in what follows some fundamental aspects of characterizing a network are presented. Particular attention will be devoted to aspects pertaining to *contagion*, which will be the central topic in the following chapters.

1.1.1 Edges characteristics

1.1.1.1 Direction

Consider the networks of Facebook (Figure 1.1a) and X (Figure 1.1b) accounts. In both cases, a node is an account on an online service, typically representing an individual user of the service. The edges, however, are of a very different nature: in order to become friends on Facebook, two people must both agree and accept, while becoming a follower of someone on X is a one-sided interaction. This is an important aspect of the network to take into account: in practical terms, this means that when recording the presence of an edge between two X accounts, we also want to record the *direction* of the edge, or who is following whom. We call such networks *directed*, and networks such as the one of friendship over Facebook, where the relationship is symmetric, *undirected*.

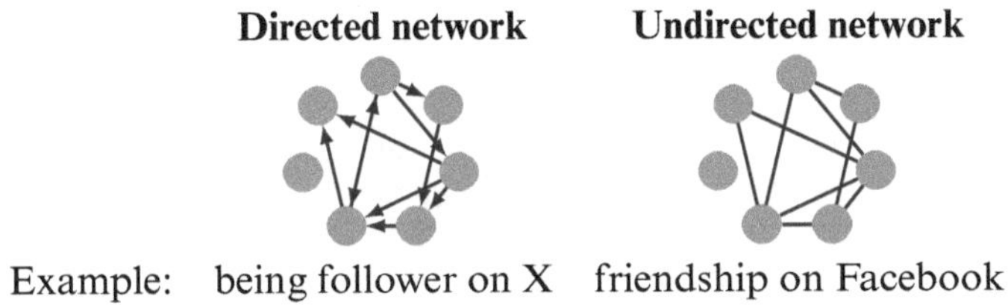

Figure 1.2 Directed/Undirected network

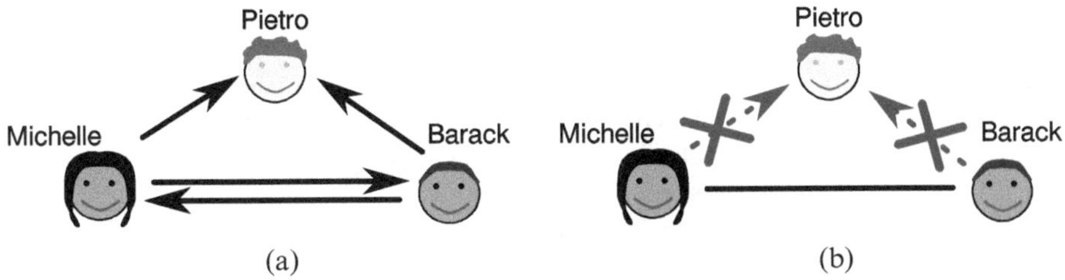

Figure 1.3 (a): X followers; (b): Facebook friends

If Barack and Michelle are friends, and they both have a X account, then it is fairly plausible that Michelle's account is following Barack's account, and vice versa. In the description of a directed network, these will figure as two distinct edges, one in each direction. There might also be a third X account, say of Pietro, which follows Barack's account but is not followed back by Barack's account (Figure 1.3a). Alternatively, if Barack and Michelle are friends on Facebook (an undirected network), there is a single edge between their profiles; if Barack and Pietro do not both accept each other as a friend, there cannot be any edge between them (Figure 1.3b).

1.1.1.2 Weight

Networks in Figure 1.1c and Figure 1.1g were both recorded by researchers studying social relations, although of different natures, and between fairly different categories of subjects. Researchers who drew the former were studying the social relations of sharks: by placing acoustic transmitters on the fins of the animals, they were able to track their movements within a large area of the central Pacific Ocean over a period of three years, making it possible to measure the extent to which and how often groups of two or more sharks could be observed — or, better, heard — together. The data used to produce Figure 1.1g, instead, was assembled by researchers who asked all students at an American high school to identify, among all their school mates, those with whom they had had a 'romantic or sexual' relationship in the previous 18 months.[4] Both networks hence describe some sort of relationship between subjects, but the main difference between the two representations (from the perspective of network theory!) is that while, in the former, thicker edges connect pairs of

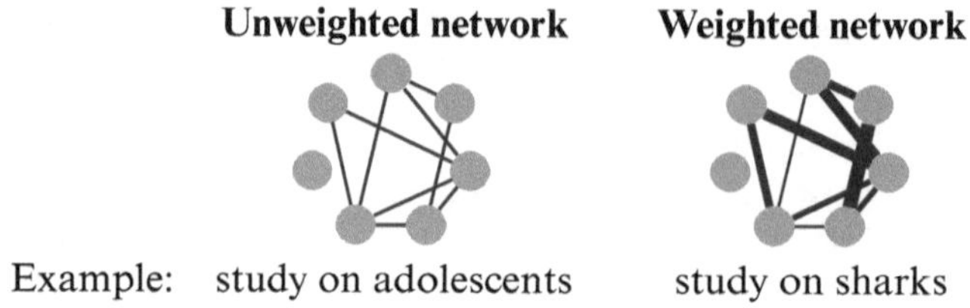

Figure 1.4 Weighted/Unweighted network

sharks detected together on multiple occasions, all edges look similar in the representation of the adolescents' network. That is, the representation of the sharks' network, but not that of the students' network, conveys a measure of the *intensity* of the relationships being analyzed.

When recording a network, it is possible to account for the intensity of a relationship by attaching to each edge a number called '*weight*'; hence we say that the sharks' network is a *weighted* network, and the 'heavier' the relationship between two nodes, the thicker will the line connecting them typically be drawn.

The weights assigned to edges can sometimes have different interpretations than the intensity of a relationship: for instance, if the network represents the roads between cities in the world, with each node corresponding to a city and each edge to a road, then we could associate to each road its *length*. If the network represents the lines of a train system, with each node representing a station, it could be interesting to associate each edge with the *cost* of traveling over it. If instead the network represents connections between computers and servers on the internet, it could be informative to associate each edge with the *bandwidth* of a given connection.

The presence, and interpretation, of weights in networks often depends on how they were recorded. In the case of the study on adolescents, for instance, the researchers asked the subjects to state the start and end date of each relationship, so its length can be interpreted as a weight. Alternatively, the researchers studying sharks could have simply defined 'shark friendship' as being observed at least once a week, resulting in an unweighted network of social relations between sharks.

In other cases, however, there is really no purpose in assigning weights to network edges. Consider the case of X, for instance: 'being a follower of someone' is a very standard kind of relationship, which can hardly be attributed a weight. Does this mean that all relationships on X are equal? It depends on what we mean by 'equal'. If Barack and Michelle are two public persona, the fact that they are following each other on X — or not — might make the news and be considered 'important'. If then Barack then starts to follow Pietro, a less famous scholar, this could also be an 'important' fact, at least for Pietro. But this is not because of the *structure of the relationship*, that is, the intensity with which Barack clicked the 'follow' button. What makes the edge important are the characteristics of the *nodes* connected by it — the fact that Barack was important from the outset.

1.1.2 Nodes characteristics

1.1.2.1 Imputing importance

Not all edges in a network are equal, and the same can be said of nodes. Consider a network of banks (Figure 1.1h), where two banks are connected if there is a loan between them. It is a strongly heterogeneous network, where huge banks with billions of US dollars in capitalization and millions of customers coexist and interact with small, often local banks. Capitalization is indeed the typical way to quickly measure the importance of a bank, and it is information often considered in any kind of analysis of banking networks. In the example in Figure 1.1h, nodes are drawn of different sizes to reflect the capitalization of the different banks.

Now let us consider again the network of X accounts. On December 2, 2017, in a talk in New Delhi, former US president Barack Obama made a jab concerning his X (then Twitter) followers (97 million, making his account the third most followed overall at the time): he had, he said, 'more than other people who use it more often' (the reference clearly being to current president Donald Trump, who 'only' had 44 million followers).[5] Despite having done so half–jokingly, Obama followed the widespread custom of mentioning the number of followers as a measure of *importance*, or *success*, on X.

So, should we expect capitalization for banks and number of followers for X accounts to play similar roles (measuring importance) in our analysis of the respective networks? Not really. True, the number of followers is often used as a metric of importance, but such metrics *originate* from the network of followers, and do not add anything to it. On the contrary, while larger banks typically have more connections to other banks, there might also be relatively isolated large banks and relatively well connected small banks. In other words, capitalization is a feature of the node itself (the bank), not a description of the position of the node in the network (as with a user's X followers).

This is why it makes sense to draw the X network as composed by homogeneous nodes (see Figure 1.5): intuitively, drawing larger circles for nodes with more followers would not convey any additional information beyond what the lines, or edges, already convey.

This distinction is critical because researchers often want to identify important nodes, or groups of nodes, when studying a network. In cases such as the banking network, researchers employ external information (about nodes) with which they can *complement* the network structure; alternatively, in cases such as the X network, they mainly look for ways to extract information *from* the network structure. Note that an X account could possibly be considered more important if the user posts more often, or if its posts are on average longer. But this just does not seem — both to journalists and to researchers who analyze

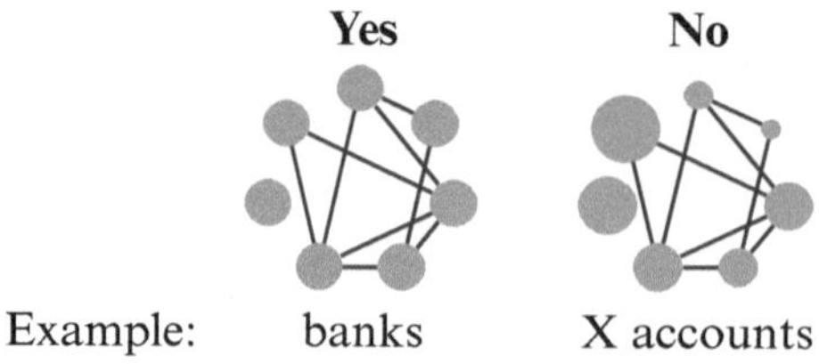

Figure 1.5 External measure of importance

the X network — as interesting as the number of followers, in part because producing more or longer tweets is trivial, while gaining followers, as we will see in Chapter 4, is ... slightly less trivial.

We have seen that, in a given network, there might be different ways to assign edge weights, allowing for the study of different phenomena, and the same is true for node weights. The banking network reveals which bank has financial relationships with other banks, and by combining this with capitalization, researchers could answer the question, 'Are the biggest banks also the most active in the interbank market?' But if, for instance, researchers wanted to know how a shock in oil prices would affect the banking system, they could instead have the node size reflect a bank's investment in the oil-related industry and could answer a question such as 'Do banks which finance oil firms interact more frequently among themselves than with other banks?'

1.1.2.2 Space

In the (directed, weighted) network of Figure 1.1i, each edge represents the number of migrants moving between municipalities in China. It shares with Figure 1.1j one characteristic that distinguishes both networks, even visually, from all other examples: each node occupies a specific and unique position in space (see Figure 1.6). This can be an important element for the analysis because, for instance, individuals might relocate more easily from Tianjin to Beijing, just 120 kilometers away, than from Tianjin to Shenzhen, located in the southern part of the country. Hence, one might expect the distance between two cities to reflect negatively on the weight of the edge connecting them.

The spatial disposition of nodes in some cases will even determine the possibility or impossibility of the *existence* of specific edges. For instance, Miami and Havana are just 367 kilometers apart (compared to the 634 kilometers between Washington and Boston), but the presence of the Caribbean Sea makes the planning of a highway connection between them at least implausible. Alternatively, in the case of actors (Figure 1.1k), many of whom probably live in the Hollywood area or have relocated several times during their career, the importance of geographic position at a given moment in time in explaining collaborations can probably be considered close to irrelevant. In other cases, connecting the different nodes might require specific technical expedients; for

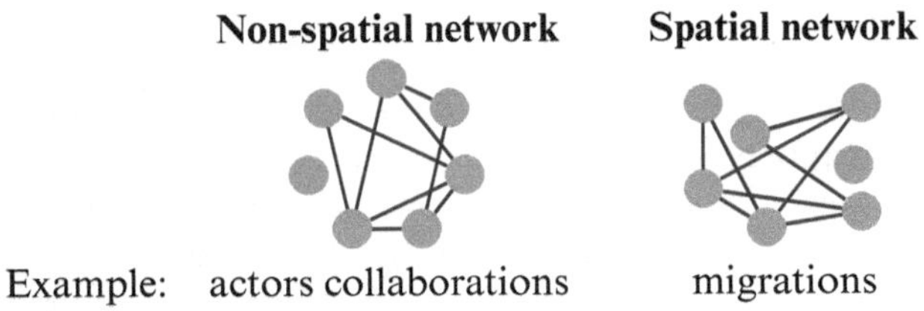

Figure 1.6 Spatial/Non-spatial network

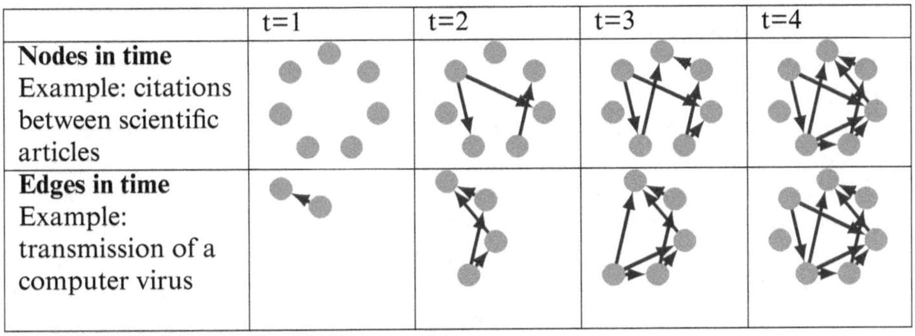

Figure 1.7 Possible growth modes of a network

instance, since electric tracks in a printed circuit board (Figure 1.1l) cannot cross each other, multilayer boards are typically required in order to build complex electronic circuits.

1.1.2.3 Time

There is one last ingredient that can be crucial for understanding networks, and which can characterize both nodes and edges: *time* (see Figure 1.7). Consider, for instance, Figure 1.1m, where nodes are scientific articles, and there is an edge from one article to another if the first article contains a citation to the second. Given that scientific articles are fundamentally immutable (only in rare circumstances corrections are made on an article after it is published, and they typically do not alter its list of citations), we know an edge can only go from one article to another one that was published *previously*. This is an obvious way in which time–tagging each *node* can tell us something about the structure of a network. Alternatively, consider the diffusion of a computer virus inside a big firm, where nodes represent computers and each edge denotes the passage of the virus from one device to another. Time–tagging each *edge* allows us to reconstruct where the infection started, and how it propagated. So, depending on the nature of the network under analysis, it can be useful to associate a specific moment in time to each node, or to each edge, or both.

1.2 Network measures

When a child learns to draw, people around him in his daily life will likely be among the first subjects represented, and the first representations will *enumerate* their common features: two legs, two arms, one head. Soon after, the child will discover which elements *differentiate* them: that mum has long hair, say, that dad has a beard, or that his older sister has a ball. If the child, several years later, pursues a career as a painter, he will probably take a class in anatomy, learning more advanced techniques for drawing both *credible* and *recognizable* portraits.

Like portraitists, medical doctors must also study the human body, but from a very different angle. In order to make a *diagnosis* concerning a human body, a doctor will be less concerned with the patient's height and even less with the color of the patient's hair, or the length of the patient's nails. Rather, she will *measure* aspects that are less evident on the exterior, but nonetheless vital, such as blood pressure, pulse, and any noise produced when breathing. The measures discussed thus far provide the tools to recognize and describe a network based on its external qualities, but what about the 'inner workings' of networks?

In some cases, a quick glance at the graphic representation of a network provides enough information to detect interesting phenomena or patterns (Figure 1.1i does suggest that people tend to move to closer cities rather than to further ones); but in other cases (consider Figure 1.1n), the representation may look more like contemporary art than as a way to convey any factual information about a specific phenomenon.

In what follows, we will see certain measures that are meant to characterize individual nodes or pairs of nodes — a bit like a doctor who analyzes cells taken from a blood sampling — and can serve as the basis for measures that instead look at *entire networks* at once.

1.2.1 Measuring nodes

Twitter (now X) has only existed since 2006, but the habit of qualifying X accounts based on number of followers was nothing new to network scientists. They had long considered the number of edges attached to a node a measure of its importance. In this spirit, a shark is more social if it interacts with a higher number of other sharks, and the number of edges of each node (students) in Figure 1.1g might be an indication of promiscuity, in the sense of having a larger number of partners in a given time span. In general, the *degree* of a node is the number of edges attached to it.

This simple definition must be adapted, however, to the different typologies of networks previously presented. In the X network, knowing that a node has one hundred outgoing edges (followers) reveals something very different from knowing it has one hundred incoming edges (*followed* accounts). Hence, in all directed networks, it is important to distinguish between the *indegree* (number of incoming links) and the *outdegree* (number of outgoing links).

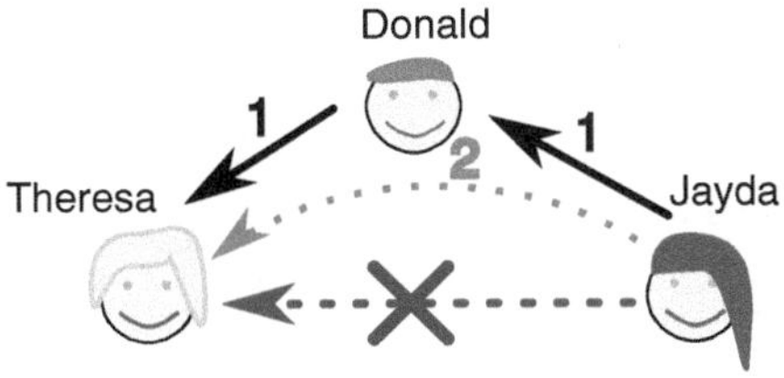

Figure 1.8 A network of three X users

Moreover, in weighted networks, such as the network of social relations between sharks, the mere count of edges attached to a given node can be of limited interest: over a sufficiently long period of time, any two sharks in the population of 44 subjects might approach each other at least once, and in this case the degree of each node would be 43. Summing together the *weights* of the links attached to a node will provide a more interesting measure of whether a given shark is particularly social or isolated: this is the *weighted* degree of a node. In weighted *and* directed networks, the weighted indegree and outdegree will typically be the most immediate ways to characterize a network. So, for instance, in Figure 1.1i, the weighted indegree of a city, when compared to its population, is a rough measure of its attractiveness, while a city with a large weighted outdegree might be facing an economic downturn.

Looking at *pairs* of nodes, then, is a bit like looking at the basic interaction between pairs of cells, or organs, in the human body. We know that when two nodes are connected by an edge, this (and, in some cases, the direction and weight of the edge), informs us about some relation between them. But how can we tell something about a *generic* — not necessarily connected — pair of nodes? One simple way is to look at their *distance*, that is, the minimum number of edges (or *hops*) required to go from one to the other. For instance, even though Theresa does not directly follow Jayda's X account in Figure 1.8, as long as she follows Donald's account and Donald follows Jayda (that is, Theresa is at distance of two from Jayda), then it is likely that Theresa occasionally sees tweets from Jayda (for example, if Donald happens to retweet some of them). This example also explains the way arrows were drawn in Figure 1.8, *from* the followee *to* the follower; hence reflecting not the direction of the 'following' action, but rather the flow of information to which this connection can lead: if Theresa follows Donald, then the content of Donald's tweets will 'flow' to Theresa's.

In some cases, there might be *no path* — that is, sequence of edges from one node to another. In Figure 1.1g of romantic or sexual relationships between students, *most* pairs of nodes have no path connecting them. For instance, there are sixty–three couples of adolescents who reported only having a relationship with each other, which means they are disconnected from any other node. When there is no path from one node to another, the distance between the two nodes is considered *infinite*. In fact, even the example in Figure 1.8 is not as simple as it might seem. The distance from Jayda to Theresa is indeed two, but what is the distance *from* Theresa *to* Jayda? It is infinite, because there is actually no edge (and hence path) from Theresa to any other node since Donald does not follow Theresa's account and Jayda does not follow Donald's account.

1.2.2 From local to global measures

The degree is a *local* measure; like a magnifying glass, it provides information on the smallest possible part of a network: a node. There are other measures — some of which will appear later in this book – that look beyond a single node while still restricting attention to small parts of the network; for instance, considering two or three adjacent nodes at a time.

Global measures, instead, provide information on an entire network. In this sense, the distance between two nodes is already very different from the degree of a node: not simply because it considers two nodes at a time rather than one, but because while doing so, it necessarily takes into consideration *other* nodes in the network — it is actually *not* local. Figure 1.8 provides the simplest possible example of this: if we want to measure the distance from Jayda and Theresa, we need to also take into account Donald. When two nodes are at a larger distance from each other, then, more nodes are involved in providing a path between them: knowing that two nodes are distant provides important information on the network they are inside.

Both these measures — the degree of a node and the distance between two nodes — can then be extended to (global) measures that seek to describe an entire network with a single number.

How many followers does a *typical* X account have? How many links are there among existing web pages? How many roads must a man walk down, before you can claim he has walked the entire New York road system? The answer to all these questions is similar and amounts to determining how many edges are in a given network.

Often, however, the sheer number of edges is not very informative. Knowing that there are more edges in the network of web pages, which contains millions of nodes, than the network of adolescents in the high school, which totals 573, is of limited interest. More interesting would be to know what share of the *theoretically possible* edges — given the nodes — exist. Luckily, this is not difficult to determine.

Consider again the X accounts of Theresa, Donald, and Jayda. If each of them was following each other, this small network would have no more than $3 \times 2 = 6$ edges. More generally, a network with N nodes cannot possibly have more than $N \times (N-1) = N^2 - N$ edges.[6] Now, in order to have a measure of how connected a network is, we just divide the *actual* number of edges by this upper bound. If the network contains no edges, we obtain $\frac{0}{N^2-N} = 0$. If instead all possible edges are present, we obtain $\frac{N^2-N}{N^2-N} = 1$. In the example represented above, where Theresa is a follower of Donald and Donald is a follower of Jayda, we have $\frac{2}{6} = \frac{1}{3}$.

Things change slightly if we are considering an *undirected* network, such as Facebook, because the count above would include twice each edge (for example, the friendship between Barack and Michelle, *and* between Michelle and Barack). In such networks, the maximum possible number of edges is equal to the number of possible pairs of nodes, which is *half* of what it is in directed networks: $\frac{N^2-N}{2}$. So for instance if Barack and Michelle are friends on Facebook, but they are not friends with Pietro, there is only one link, out of $\frac{9-3}{2} = 3$ possible links — that is, the proportion of actual links over possible links is again $\frac{1}{3}$.

In general, this proportion between actual and possible edges — which is always a number between 0 and 1 — is called the *density* of a network. Returning to the comparison between the network of web pages and the network of adolescents, the number of edges is much larger in the case of the web pages, but it can be shown to have much lower density (the overwhelming majority of pairs of web pages are not linked among them). Indeed, a network's density depends on its nodes' degrees but, given nodes with similar degrees, a larger network will have lower density. To see why, consider that when Facebook reached the 1000 users mark (within the first 24 hours after it was launched, in February 2004),[7] having one friendship relation per user was already enough to guarantee a density of the friendship network of at least 0.1% — that is, every 1000 possible edges, at least one actually existed. When Facebook passed the 1 billion users mark (on October 4, 2012), in order to reach an overall density of 0.1% the average degree should have reached the highly implausible value of *one million*. Density is determined by, but is not equal to, average degree.

As will be made clear in the following chapters, sometimes the density of a network is an important element not just to *describe* the network, and *compare* it to other networks, but also to predict phenomena that take place *on* the network.

For the moment, recall the promise made at the end of the previous section: that the first two measures encountered — degree and distance — would be the basis for two global measures of an entire network. Indeed, we have defined density as the total number of edges divided by the maximum possible number of edges, but the total number of edges is simply the sum of the *degrees* of all nodes divided by two. But is it the sum of *degrees*, *out*degrees, or *in*degrees? In undirected networks, there is only the degree; in directed networks instead, any of the out- and indegree will do the job, as their sum is always the same (any edge which starts from a node must necessarily end at some other node).

Now consider the *average distance* between nodes (that is, in hops). The task can seem burdensome but it is in principle quite simple. In an undirected network, we list all the pairs of nodes (which we now know to be $\frac{N^2-N}{2}$) and sum together all the distances between nodes in each pair (let's say that *there is* a path from any node to any other node). Then we divide the result by $\frac{N^2-N}{2}$.

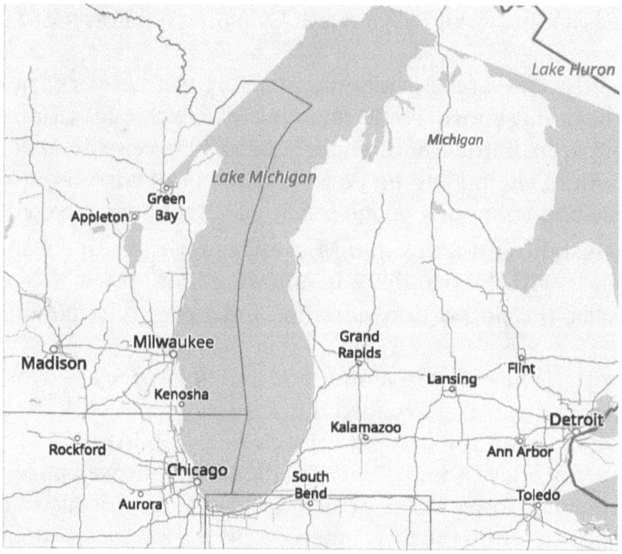

Figure 1.9 A map of the area around Lake Michigan

In a directed network, the principle is the same, except that we consider both distances between each of the two nodes (from Jayda to Theresa, from Theresa to Jayda) and divide the sum by $N^2 - N$.

Another global measure related to the average distance, but perhaps more intuitive, begins again with calculating the distances between all pairs of nodes: but instead of taking their mean, we then look for the *largest* distance. The *diameter* of the network is the distance between the two nodes that are furthest away one from the other. In many cases, the average distance and the diameter of a network tell us more or less the same thing: after all, if nodes in a network tend to be *close* to each other, then typically the two furthest away from each other will not be that far — and vice versa. But still, the most appropriate measure depends on the question being asked about a network.

Are these two global measures of networks — density and average distance — somehow related?

To answer, consider the road network in the United States, where every city is a node. No direct road connects Milwaukee, Wisconsin, to Grand Rapids, Michigan, simply because Lake Michigan extends between them (see Figure 1.9). To ride from one to the other, one typically must travel through a portion of Indiana and then through the urban area of Chicago. What would happen to density and average distance of the network if a tunnel were built directly connecting the two cities? Referring back at the formula for calculating the density, we see it would increase, because the number of edges would increase by one while the total number of nodes — and hence of *possible* edges — would be left unchanged. The distance between *most* pairs of cities in the United States (say,

San Francisco and Sacramento) would be left unchanged, but it would decrease for some pairs (both in kilometers, and in hops). For instance, the network distance between Grand Rapids and Milwaukee would now be one. And in general, this is what happens: all else equal, when the number of edges increases, the distances decrease. But what does *'all else equal'* actually mean? This question opens the door to some of the most interesting concepts of networks theory. It is true that if we take *any* network and add *any* edge, we increase the density and decrease the average distance. But we will soon see that the interplay between density and average distance when comparing *different* networks is far from trivial.

For the moment, we will conclude this section with a few more measures that allow us to describe the entire structure of the network, and at the same time give an intuition of single node characteristics.

1.2.3 Clustering and assortativity

If we randomly pick two Facebook accounts, what is the probability that there is an edge between them — that is, that they are friends? The answer to this question is just the density of the Facebook friendship network, and even without knowing the exact number of existing accounts and the average number of friends, we can easily guess that this probability is pretty low (most people with an account on Facebook are *not* friends with each other).

But if we randomly pick one account on Facebook and then two of its friends, what is the probability that those two friends are also friends themselves? This time, the likelihood is pretty high. It is important to note that if Facebook users chose their (Facebook) friends at random from all available accounts, the answer would still be 'the density of the network'. Instead it is a fact that, in many real–world networks, two neighbors of a given node are often neighbors themselves (more often than two random nodes). This property is called 'clustering', the idea being that a network is made of clusters: communities of nodes in which neighbors of neighbors are often neighbors themselves.

Given a specific Facebook account, we can look at its friends and determine how many of them (more precisely, what share of the pairs of friends) are friends themselves. This 'clustering coefficient', which is always a number between zero and one, can reveal a lot about a node. For instance, if all students in a school class are friends on Facebook, and one student has *no* Facebook friends outside the class, then his clustering coefficient is 1. Alternatively, a flight attendant who regularly travels across the globe and befriends people who live far apart will typically have friends who are not friends themselves, and hence her clustering coefficient will be close to 0.

Once again, a local measure forms the basis for a global one: by taking the average clustering coefficient across all nodes (add them all together and divide by the number of nodes), we obtain a *global* clustering coefficient. Like the local version, the global version of the clustering coefficient is always a number between zero (the clustering coefficient of the star–shaped network in

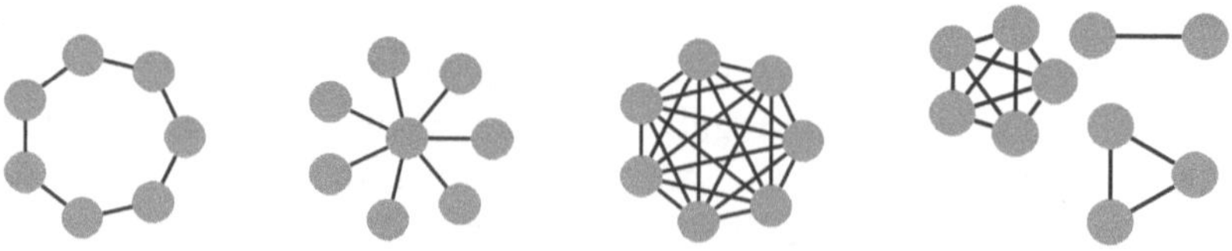

Figure 1.10 Basic network structures

Figure 1.10b) and one (the clustering coefficient of the complete network in Figure 1.10c), where a larger number implies more closely knit communities, separated from one another.

It is worth noting another aspect that distinguishes the star-shaped network from the complete network, an aspect which will play a fundamental role in Chapter 5. The complete network (just like most networks in Figure 1.1) includes a large number of *loops*, that is, sequences of edges that start at a node and come back to the same node through a circular path. Instead, there is no loop at all in the star-like network (and there is only one in the circle-like network, which also has a clustering coefficient equal to zero).

Consider now the Facebook profiles of two friends, Emmanuel and Matteo. Facebook profiles have on average 155 friends,[8] and we happen to know that Emmanuel has 200. Can we guess whether his friend Matteo has more or less than the average 155 friends? Clearly we do not know, but we can argue what we *expect* the answer to be given two random Facebook profiles. That is, we can ask: do friends of people with many friends tend to also have many friends? Or in network terms, do nodes with large degrees tend to be connected to nodes with large degrees? The answer to this question is generally far from obvious. It is yes for the Facebook network,[9] as indeed users with many friends tend to be friends with users with many friends. However, there are real-world networks in which the opposite holds true.

Consider the network of routers (nodes) and cables (edges) that form the internet, and allow users to transmit and receive information all over the globe. It is an undirected network and a fascinating topic for scholars working on networks, given the difficulty of its task (connecting billions of users with heterogeneous requirements) and its strong level of decentralization (routers are operated by a large number of independent entities). Last time I tried to access the Columbia University website (www.columbia.edu) from my home in Pisa, Tuscany, Italy, my request went through eighteen different routers.[10] The first of these was my own router, which is operated by me and is connected to only one other router, operated by the internet service provider from which I purchase Internet access. That second router, however, provides internet access to dozens, or hundreds, of other customers. This pattern is not an exception: when a router is attached to just one other router, then this one router is often attached to many. Or in other words, nodes with large degrees tend to be connected to nodes with small degrees.

The *assortativity* of a network is the tendency of nodes that are similar among them — for instance in terms of degree — to be connected.[11] It is a number between negative one (the assortativity of degrees in a star network, as represented in Figure 1.10b) and one (the assortativity of degrees in a network composed of separated, complete clusters, as represented in Figure 1.10d). Simply put, the network of friendship on Facebook has positive degree assortativity, while the network of internet routers has negative degree assortativity.

1.2.4 A glocal *measure*

Centrality, the last measure presented in this chapter, will play a … central role in the following chapters. As discussed previously, while measures of importance can be *attached* to nodes in a network (such as capitalization for banks), in many cases such measures will be extracted *from* the network (this was the case for the number of followers in the X network). One obvious way to do this (again, in the X network, for instance) is by determining the (out)*degree*. But centrality is a slightly more sophisticated tool, which researchers often rely on in order to get a sense of the importance of a given node *taking into consideration the entire network*, rather than just neighbor nodes. Like the number of X followers, centrality allows for the evaluation of node significance in a purely network — driven way — based on the structure of the network, not on external information. In fact, strictly speaking, centrality is not even a measure, but rather a concept so important in the field of networks, that *several* well-known measures of it have been proposed.

The basic idea is, once again, simple: we know that in many networks in Figure 1.1, nodes with more connections are considered more important. Indeed, the degree of a node provides a hint about how well connected a node is to the rest of the network. Now, consider two web pages, A and B, each linked from three other pages and without any outgoing links, meaning A and B have both the same indegree, and the same outdegree (Figure 1.11). However, the three pages linking page A have themselves no incoming links, while page B is linked from the homepage of Wikipedia, from the biography of the president on the White House website, and from the description of a very popular video on YouTube. Clearly, if we wanted to rank web pages according to their position in the network of the World Wide Web (not a completely foolish idea, as we will soon see), page B would be considered 'better placed' than page A … or more *central*. While the degree of a node only communicates something about its *immediate* neighbors, the goal of centrality measures is to evaluate the position of a node by looking *further than* distance one. Interestingly, we do not need to refer to external measures of importance to state that the homepage of Wikipedia, the biography of the president on the White House website, and the popular video on YouTube are important pages. We will just reapply the same

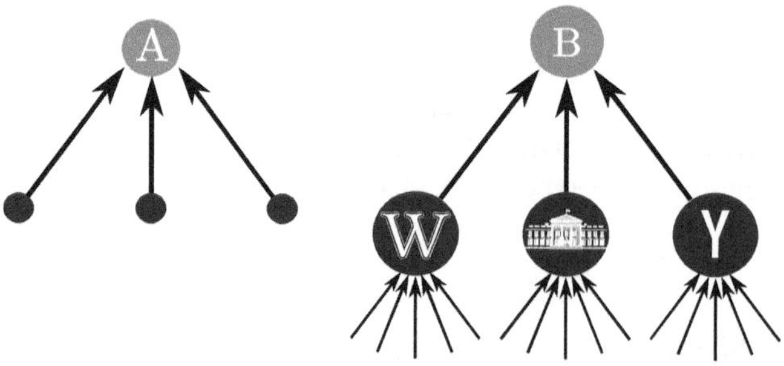

Figure 1.11 Two very different web pages with the same indegree

principle applied to pages A and B — that is, the intuition that a page is central if *its neighbors* are numerous *and* also central.

One popular and simple measure of centrality is *betweenness centrality*. Assume that we take the phone book of some small town in the French countryside and start visiting random addresses picked from it. We begin by going to the first address, then we pick another and walk to the next address, and so on. Each time, we follow the shortest path from the previous address to the next. Which places will we see most often in a full day of this activity? Probably the main square of the town, where the old church and council hall sit. This is because such a square is *central*, and many paths between two places in the town pass through it. This is the essence of betweenness centrality: taking all pairs of nodes and determining the shortest path (clearly in network terms — that is, in hops) between them. Then, we consider all these 'shortest paths' and count how many of them pass through a given node.[12] For instance, the star network in Figure 1.10b is a bit similar to the French town: the center node has a betweenness centrality of one and all the others have a betweenness centrality of zero. In the circle network of Figure 1.10a, instead, no node is more *central* than the others, and indeed, they all have a centrality of $\frac{1}{5}$.

There is an even more direct way to exploit distance between nodes to determine centrality. In the French town, we could for instance wonder whether a given address is in a position such that it is not too far away from most other addresses – probably finding out that this holds for the central square. Specifically, we can measure *closeness* on a network as the reciprocal of distance, so that two nodes which are six steps away would be considered '$\frac{1}{6}$ close'. Then, we could look at how close, on average, is a given node to all other nodes, hence measuring its *closeness centrality*. In Figure 1.10b the center node would be assigned a centrality of one, and all other nodes a lower centrality ($\frac{8}{14}$). Once more, all nodes in Figure 1.10a would instead be assigned the same centrality ($\frac{11}{21}$).

A measure of centrality which is notable for having entered the jargon of many practitioners is *PageRank* centrality. While its calculation is less obvious than betweenness centrality, the intuition is simple: imagine a web surfer who

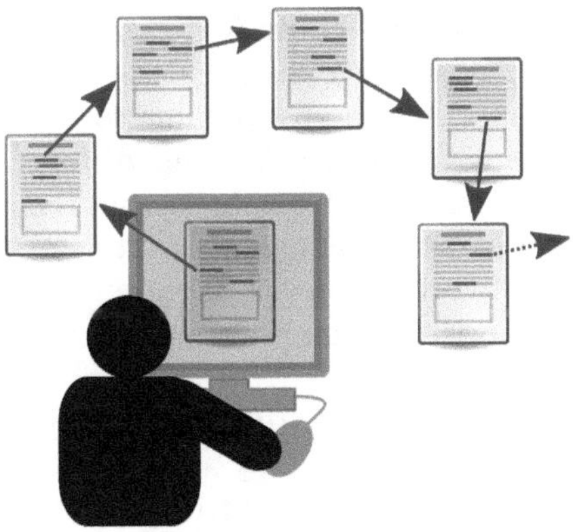

Figure 1.12 The random surfer

starts on a random page, clicks one random link on that page, and goes on for years clicking random links on the pages he visits, as depicted in Figure 1.12. What is the probability that after exactly ten years he will be looking at a given page? It clearly depends on the number of links pointing to that page, but also on the number of links pointing to pages that link to that page, and so on. The PageRank centrality measure was the main driving factor for the success of the Google search engine, which, when launched in 1997, quickly overcame the competition thanks to its ability to rank search results in order of importance, rather than just based on page content (for example, the number of times they featured the desired given keywords). The ability to extract a measure of importance *from the network of links* was the essential strength of the new search engine.

Other measures of centrality exist, such as eigenvector centrality (a close relative to PageRank centrality) and Katz centrality (again similar to PageRank centrality, but potentially more useful in scarcely connected networks). They all serve a similar purpose — extracting a measure of the importance of specific nodes from the network — but a thorough technical discussion of the differences is outside of the scope of this book. Suffice it to say that centrality measures have been adapted to weighted, directed, and time–changing networks, and have assumed a fundamental role in many different fields to which networks theory has been applied.

1.3 Small global networks

Consider an undirected network of three nodes: as long as no node is isolated from the others, the diameter cannot possibly be larger than two, and the average distance cannot be larger than $\frac{4}{3}$. If nodes are gradually added to the network, connecting them to the existing ones, both the diameter and the average distance can increase. In general, networks composed of a large number of nodes can have a larger diameter, and average distance, than networks with only a handful of nodes. For instance, our body contains several long chain–shaped molecules (Figure 1.1o) with a very large average distance and diameter — almost as large as their maximum possible values given the number of nodes–atoms. However, an intriguing result emerged over the years from the analysis of several different kinds of networks: even very large networks can be 'small worlds', in the sense of having surprisingly small average distances and diameters.[13]

Frigyes Karinthy, a Hungarian writer, was probably the first to propose, in 1929, the idea that any two human beings are connected by a chain of 'friends of friends' of at most six steps[14] (that is, that the network of friendship between humans has a diameter no larger than six). Several attempts were made over the years to substantiate this suggestive idea with hard facts. Of note were the 'small world experiments' carried out by social psychologist Stanley Milgram and other researchers. In 1967, they sent packages to random people in the United States, and asked them to return the packages to a specific individual in Boston, Massachusetts, by only passing them to people they personally knew. The researchers lost track of most of the packages, but they observed that those that finally arrived at the intended destination took on average *a bit less* than six steps. To some extent, this supported the 'small world' theory, but clearly it was possible that lost packages were precisely those lacking a quick path of acquaintances to the destination, distorting the results. On the other hand, while some packages took as many as ten links to reach their destination, it could be argued that participants in the experiment did not actually know which path would have been the shortest, and they had to guess which of their acquaintances would be a better fit for forwarding the package. The Columbia Small World Project was an analogous attempt run through e–mail in 2003. While it confirmed that most 'visible' chains were short, it was plagued by the same two main limitations on Milgram's version: the large number of broken chains, and the impossibility for participants to really know for sure which was the optimal path to take among their acquaintances.

In the meantime, other large networks had proven to be surprisingly small.

Paul Erdős (1913–1996) was a Hungarian mathematician famous not just for his cleverness and breadth of scientific interests (including the field of graph theory — the branch of mathematics on which the theory of networks is based), but also for transforming such eclecticism into an impressive number of scientific publications, written with an even more impressive number of collaborators. During his career, he authored more than 1,500 publications (for a mathematician, one hundred publications can already be considered a lifetime achievement) in collaboration with more than 500 coauthors from several countries. Considering all of this, an inside joke started to spread among his friends: the so-called *Erdős number*. A researcher's Erdős number is simply the distance from Erdős in the network of scientific collaboration (Figure 1.1p): so it is zero if he is Paul Erdős, one if he or she published a paper with Erdős, two if he or she published a paper with an author whose Erdős number is one, and so on.

Paul Erdős died in 1996, but today it is still common for mathematicians to know their own Erdős number, and in some cases to display it proudly on their personal web page. Most importantly — for our purposes — among the thousands of mathematicians active around the world in the last century or so, the majority can be shown to have an Erdős number below five. And while the fact that Fields medalists (the closest equivalent to Nobel Prizes for mathematics) have an average Erdős number of 3.52 might not be surprising (after all, awardees are mathematicians who can be expected to have core positions in the networks of collaborations), less expected is the fact that the average Erdős number of Nobel laureates in *physics* and *economics* is 4.42 and 4.91, respectively, still very small numbers.

In 1994, three college students developed a similar game based on the network of collaboration between Hollywood actors (Figure 1.1k): the 'six degrees of Kevin Bacon'. Similar to the Erdős number, the underlying idea is to show that each actor present in the network is close to Kevin Bacon (presumably chosen for having played in more than eighty movies, with hundreds of other actors). Among the actors who can be linked to Kevin Bacon (392,732 as of March 2020), the average Kevin Bacon number is just 3.153.[15]

The Erdős number and the Kevin Bacon number have been easily computed since at least the beginning of the 1990s, because they refer to well defined communities — mathematicians and movie actors, respectively — and because the work of such communities is well documented through digital archives. In particular, the American Mathematical Society provides a tool[16] based on its bibliographic database to determine the Erdős number of any mathematician, while the Oracle of Bacon website allows visitors to identify the Kevin Bacon number of any actor present in the Internet Movie Database. This overcomes the two main issues affecting social experiments such as the ones by Milgram and researchers at Columbia: shortest paths are calculated automatically and not left to the guesswork of experiment participants. Hence, the evidence coming from these two very special communities was soon seen as suggestive and exciting — although support for the 'six degrees hypothesis' in the more general network of friendship was still debatable. Unfortunately, it was unfeasible for researchers to ask people from all around the world to register the identity of all their friends in a database.

Somewhat luckily, at least from the point of view of this field of research, things began to quickly change in 2004, as millions of people from all around the world started to *voluntarily* register in a database the identity of their friends, without any effort on behalf of social researchers: this database is called Facebook. And in November 2011 Facebook researchers announced that the average distance between users was just 4.74. Perhaps even more surprising, it was 4.46 — only slightly lower — among US users. The same researchers updated their results in February 2016, reporting that the average distance had *decreased* to 4.57 — this despite (or in virtue of) the fact that the number of users had, in the meantime, increased from 721 million to 1.6 billion.[17]

Most human beings do not have a Facebook account, but what would the average distance be if all humans suddenly created one and established connections with all their real–life acquaintances? Firstly, it must be noted that there are around one hundred 'uncontacted tribes' around the world[18] – indigenous people without any social ties to external civilization. Let us assume that these individuals did *not* create an account, so that all users who did *were* actually connected among them. Next it must be observed that Facebook account owners, *as of now*, are not 'random' human beings: it is plausible that they have on average more real–life social ties than Facebook-less human beings. So while we have seen that an increase in users can go hand in hand with an increase in connections and hence a decrease in distances, the entry of less connected individuals could push up the average distance. Still, one can argue that the average distance between any two humans is probably not too far from the figures released by the Facebook researchers, which are in turn not too far from the wild guess that Karinthy had made in 1929.

Small world networks are not just an intellectual curiosity. Indeed, they have profound implications for network–related phenomena that shape our daily lives. On a 'small world' network, we will see, epidemics, news, and financial distress are able to more quickly reach all the network.

Notes

1 Jacoby, Papastamatiou, and Freeman, 2016.
2 Battiston and Stanca, 2015.
3 Giovannetti et al., 2004.
4 Bearman, Moody, and Stovel, 2004.
5 https://washingtonpost.com/news/worldviews/wp/2017/12/01/obama-issues-a-warning-in-india-think-before-you-tweet
6 In some cases — X is not one of these — it makes sense to allow for nodes to be connected to themselves, for a total of potentially $N \times N$ edges. Consider, for instance, the example of industrial sectors (Figure 1.1e): firms *within* an industrial sector might trade with each other, forming an edge from the sector to itself.
7 https://theguardian.com/technology/2007/jul/25/media.newmedia
8 According to a survey — https://telegraph.co.uk/news/science/science-news/12108412/Facebook-users-have-155-friends-but-would-trust-just-four-in-a-crisis.html
9 Ugander et al., 2011.
10 Such checks can be ran with the 'traceroute' utility. Several websites are available that provide this service through a browser.
11 Formally, the assortativity coefficient is defined as the correlation between the degrees of the two nodes at the extrema of each edge.
12 The definition is easily adapted to the case in which there are *multiple* shortest paths between any two nodes.
13 Watts and Strogatz, 1998.

14 Barabasi, 2003. While several authors these days attribute the phrase to a 1909 speech by Guglielmo Marconi, no first hand evidence supporting this claim seems to be available: see Watts, 2011, p. 308.
15 http://oracleofbacon.org/onecenter.php
16 https://mathscinet.ams.org/mathscinet/freetools/collab-dist (NOT restricted to subscribers).
17 https://research.fb.com/three-and-a-half-degrees-of-separation/
18 https://newscientist.com/article/dn24090-how-many-uncontacted-tribes-are-left-in-the-world/

Bibliography

Barabasi, Albert-Laszlo (2003). 'Linked: How everything is connected to everything else and what it means'. Plume.

Battiston, Pietro and Luca Stanca (2015). 'Boundedly rational opinion dynamics in social networks: Does indegree matter?' In: *Journal of Economic Behavior & Organization* 119, pp. 400–421.

Bearman, Peter S, James Moody, and Katherine Stovel (2004). 'Chains of affection: The structure of adolescent romantic and sexual networks'. In: *American Journal of Sociology* 110.1, pp. 44–91.

Giovannetti, Manuela et al. (2004). 'Patterns of below-ground plant interconnections established by means of arbuscular mycorrhizal networks'. In: *New Phytologist*, pp. 175–181.

Jacoby, David MP, Yannis P Papastamatiou, and Robin Freeman (2016). 'Inferring animal social networks and leadership: applications for passive monitoring arrays'. In: *Journal of the Royal Society Interface* 13.124, p. 20160676.

Ugander, Johan et al. (2011). 'The anatomy of the Facebook social graph'. In: *arXiv preprint arXiv:1111.4503*.

Watts, Duncan J (2011). 'Everything is obvious: Once you know the answer'. Crown Business.

Watts, Duncan J and Steven H Strogatz (1998). 'Collective dynamics of 'small-world' networks'. In: *Nature* 393.6684, p. 440.

2 Externalities and contagion

The abilities to recognize and describe a network, both graphically and in words, are useful tools in applying the theory of networks, but they are really only the first step in taking the concept to its full potential. The Erdős number is no more than an inside joke, the clustering of the Facebook network no more than an intellectual curiosity. But armed with the knowledge of what a network is and how it is defined, researchers can explore why networks and their characteristics are important for the behavior and ultimately for the well–being of all inhabitants of planet Earth. In fact, just like the road network is important mostly by virtue of the vehicles traveling on it, most networks become only valuable when some kind of *flow* over them is identified, enabling individual nodes to affect and interact with one another.

Human beings can clearly affect the lives of other human beings in a multitude of ways, not just through social or economic networks. But an intriguing aspect of networks is that, through them, our actions often have *unintended* consequences for others, and these unintended effects are what most interest social scientists — and specifically, economists.

By way of example, consider the following question: what is the cost of driving around in one's own city for a couple of hours in one's own car? This might seem like a relatively simple question, but for an economist, it is ambiguous. What is the cost *to whom*?

The most obvious cost is the money the driver will spend for fuel. Then there is the wear and tear to tires, brakes and other parts of the car. The driver might also assign a price to the risk of having an accident, with its possible consequences on his, and his car's health. And finally, if the driver doesn't really enjoy driving, he might even quantify the cost of *not* spending that time doing something more satisfying (such as relaxing at home) — 'I would rather pay somebody twenty dollars to drive in my place'.

But these are all costs to *the driver*. This list does not include the noisy disturbance the car's engine might cause to people along the driver's route. It does not include the fact that the car will make the road slightly more congested, slowing down other drivers (the fact that they in turn slow the driver himself down does not make this less of a cost). It does not include the possible consequences

DOI: 10.4324/9781003490951-2

of an accident on *other people*'s health and cars. Nor does it include the wear and tear to the road itself, which will be borne by local taxpayers, or the emission of carbon dioxide and other pollutants with their global environmental consequences.

If the driver is only considering the costs to himself, then he will likely disregard the second list of costs to others, which do not directly impact his own well–being. Economics scholars, alternatively, who tend to focus on the *collective* well–being of societies, have always been cognizant of the plethora of ways in which our actions carry unintended costs for others — often unbeknownst to us — and designated these consequences *'negative externalities'*.

Not all unintended consequences are negative. If a neighborhood resident plants a tree in her front yard, her motivations may be strictly self–serving in that *she* likes the way the tree looks close to *her* home. However, the resident is also beautifying the entire street, which her neighbors might appreciate, and she is providing shade to pedestrians passing by in the hot summer. She is also offsetting the emissions from the driver in the previous example by converting some of the carbon dioxide released by his car back into oxygen. *Positive externalities*, such as these, do exist, but economists by and large spend more time worrying about negative externalities, possibly because it is more common to drive a car than to plant a tree (or, more generally, because it is easier to consume resources than regenerate them). Even so, often the same action causes both positive and negative externalities. If an apartment tenant spends a day listening to Bach on his stereo, with his windows open, his neighbor who likes Bach might appreciate it, while his other neighbor, who is more a fan of Handel, might be annoyed.

The concept of externalities is not particularly new. Ronald Coase, a British economist, was awarded the 1991 Nobel Prize in Economics in large part for two works on the topic, one of which dated back to 1960. The so–called 'Coase theorem' states that negative externalities are not, *in principle*, a problem: if the costs they cause are large enough, it will be sufficient to pay the person or entity responsible for them to stop; while if the costs are not so large, there is no reason to make them stop. However, reality is more complicated, and Coase was well aware of the many caveats his theorem faced when put into practice (and of the criticisms it had attracted – in his Nobel prize acceptance lecture, he referred to the theorem bearing his name as 'infamous'). His 1960 article *'The Problem of Social Cost'*[1] revolved precisely around limitations to the application of the Coase theorem.

Policy makers have always been concerned with externalities. Speed limits, compulsory vaccines, antitrust laws, green energy subsidies, bans on dirty energy, mandatory schooling, highway tolls, financial regulation — these are all fields in which externalities are among the factors considered, and sometimes the leading motivation, for regulation. There is a subtle distinction, however, between regulations justified by negative externalities and those justified by positive externalities.

Negative externalities, in which the action of one individual harms another individual, 'naturally' call for regulation because they defy the system of *rights* on which modern legal systems are based: if someone causes damage to another, he or she must pay for this. The justifications for regulations motivated by positive externalities are less obvious; these types of regulations are typically implemented in reaction to negative externalities. For instance, green energy subsidies are a reaction to the negative externality presented by pollution, and compulsory vaccines are a reaction to the negative externality presented by epidemiological contagion. In the earlier example of the tree providing shade to pedestrians, there is probably no incentive for that neighborhood resident beyond her own motivations. But there are schemes that guarantee incentives to firms planting trees *to counterbalance carbon dioxide emissions*. There is regulation deterring people from insulting each other in the street, but no regulation incentivizing them to smile at each other.

It is important to note that humans often willingly choose to pollute as little as possible, to avoid disturbing their neighbors with loud music, and to plant trees that will improve the appearance of the entire neighborhood. Indeed, economists have long been criticized for forgetting this, and for considering instead each human being as a perfectly selfish animal (a *'homo economicus'*, in the words of Italian economist Vilfredo Pareto[2]). It is true that people are to some extent responsible and altruistic, but it is also true that they do harm each other in many ways and that they typically do so unintentionally. As long as the 'problem of externalities' — both positive and negative — exists, there will be a need for economists, and governments, to attempt to find solutions.

2.1 Contagious externalities

How are externalities related to networks? When a person listens to loud music in her house, chooses not to get vaccinated, or drives recklessly, that person is not causing equal harm to everyone on a global scale. Rather, she is harming those who are *in some way* related to her: because they are her neighbors, because she interacts with them during her daily activities, or because they happen to take the same road she drives on. That is, many externalities are only possible because certain *relationships* enable them to exist. Such externalities 'occur' on a network, and they are indeed one of the main reasons why researchers are interested in networks.

This also applies to many positive externalities, one typical example being the diffusion of technologies. The messaging app WhatsApp would be useless if a person were the only user in his friend group. But if a friend of that one user installs the messaging app, he immediately benefits from being able to communicate with her. As the number of friends installing the app increases, so too does the app's value to that user. On the other hand, the total number of worldwide users is quite irrelevant to him, if nobody in his circles uses it. That is, the benefits of using a communication technology *flow* over the network of human

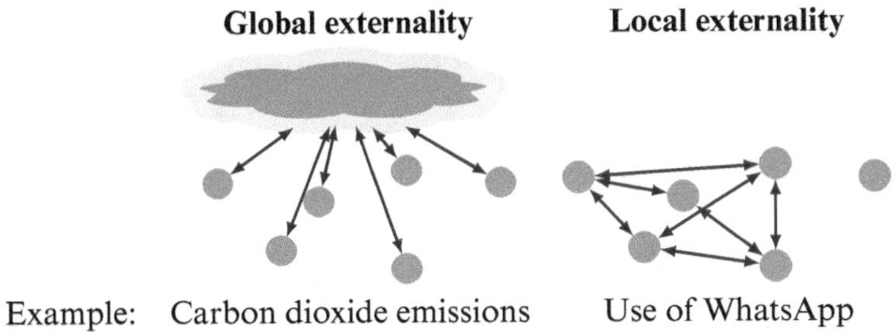

Figure 2.1 Global and local externalities

acquaintances. This applies not just to messaging apps such as WhatsApp, Telegram, Signal, and Snapchat, but also to examples that significantly predate the concept of an app, such as the telephone, email, video–conference services, and if we go even further back in time, the alphabet and language itself. In fact, the benefits of adopting a technology that is already widely in use are typically known as *network effects* — a term dating back to the Bell monopoly over US telephone services. Importantly, the adoption of a technology is typically not 'unintended'. But by installing an app, a user increases its diffusion and hence the likelihood that someone else, someone unknown to the user, benefits from it: *this* is typically unintended.

The network interpretation, however, does not fit equally well to all kinds of externalities. For instance, the main issue with carbon dioxide emissions is not that one person's engine pollutes the air specifically of *that person*'s neighbors, or friends; rather, it is the increase in the worldwide stock of carbon dioxide in the atmosphere, contributing to global warming and causing damage to other humans regardless of their 'social distance' from a single polluter (see Figure 2.1). Even so, the examples of externalities — in particular, negative ones — that occur through a network abound, and this is where the theory of networks kicks in. It help us *better understand, and tackle, externalities that affects one's neighbors through networks*.

True, the concept of externalities, and the attention of economists and policymakers to externalities, existed long before the spike of interest in network theory. For instance, while many diseases propagate through clearly defined social networks (the network of relationships in Figure 1.1g being integral to the diffusion of sexually transmitted infections), one does not necessarily need to know the structure of such a network to recommend the use of condoms. However, the ability to analyze the structure of such a network is an important tool in the hands of policy makers, and this tool becomes even more important when members of the network have at least some knowledge of the network itself, and are willing to exploit it maliciously. Two examples will be analyzed in more detail: fake news producers in Chapter 4, and financial manipulation in Chapter 5.

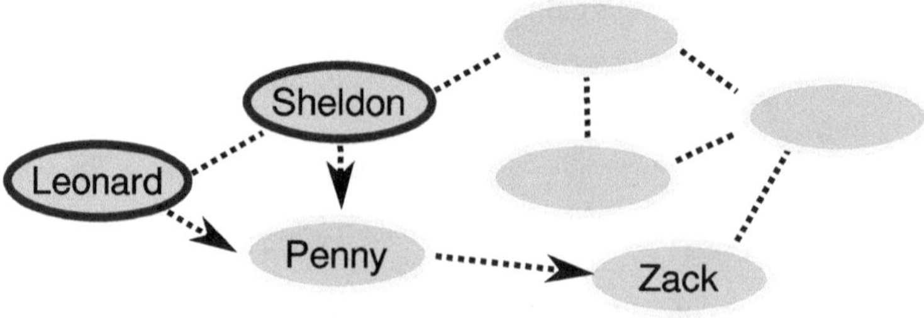

Figure 2.2 The diffusion of a hypothetical messaging app

As already mentioned, when a user installs a new messaging app on his smartphone, his friends who already use it can immediately benefit, and users whom he does not know — typically the vast majority — will not be affected. But the user's choice to install the app or not can still affect people whom he does not know personally. Consider for instance Figure 2.2, where darker nodes denote people who are already using the app. Leonard and his friend Sheldon, for instance, are early adopters. If they manage to convince their common friend Penny to install the app (because this will allow her to easily communicate with them), then not only will they benefit from being able to communicate with her, but other friends of hers (say, Zack) might also start to use the app because she does. My decision to install the app can potentially have a domino effect — through the social network — on people I am not actually connected to.

This domino effect is what network scientists often refer to as 'contagion': the idea being that, like a disease, technologies (and many other phenomena, pleasant or harmful) often *spread* over a pre–existing social network. When contagion occurs, externalities flow from node to node beyond distance 1, that is, affecting not just a node's immediate neighbors, but also their neighbors, their neighbors' neighbors, and so on. In the next chapters, we will analyze several types of contagion, including — but not limited to — epidemics, where contagion is not just a metaphor.

2.2 The structure of contagion

In most networks, calculating the degree of a node is trivial. A Facebook user's is nothing more than the number of friends; an X user's indegree and outdegree are the number of people the user follows, and the number of people who follow the user, respectively. These are measures that can be computed simply by observing one's own connections in the network — what researchers typically call one's *ego network*. We have already seen in the previous chapter, instead, that calculating the average distance in the network of acquaintances is a hard task, and the same applies to other network measures which are unfortunately crucial to understand contagion.

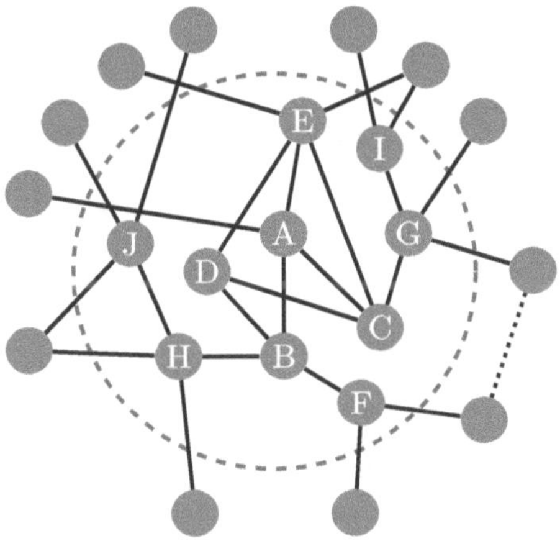

Figure 2.3 The social network of 10 hypothetical Facebook profiles — inside the smaller circle — and their friends

However, other network measures, like distance and centrality, are critical to understanding contagion; unfortunately, some of these metrics are much more difficult to quantify than simple degrees.

In order to calculate the average degree of a group of Facebook users, all one needs is access to their lists of friends: hence it can be obtained by simply visiting those pages, writing down their number of friends, and computing the mean. But calculating the average *distance* between them is much more complicated, both because the computation is less trivial, and because the amount of data needed potentially amounts to the entire Facebook network. Like in the experiments by Milgram cited in the previous chapter, finding the shortest path between any two nodes of a network is potentially complicated: repeating the operation for all possible pairs of nodes is already a significant computational effort for medium-sized networks. If, for instance, we want to calculate the average distance between nodes in the smaller circle of Figure 2.3, we will also need the list of friends of their friends (nodes in the larger circle), and of friends of their friends' friends (not shown); on Facebook, this easily amounts to millions of profiles. In fact, the work of Facebook researchers, who were able to calculate the average distance in the entire friendship network (4.57 in 2016), was made possible not just by the fact that they had access to all the social network's data, but also by the use of advanced mathematical and statistical techniques.

Unfortunately, all measures presented so far are important, even those that are not easy to compute. *There are* networks in which the degrees of nodes reveal everything we need to know, but they are relatively uninteresting. For instance, if in a town inhabitants tend to play prank phone calls to randomly composed phone numbers of the same town, consider the network in which each edge represents one of these calls in a given week. People who play more

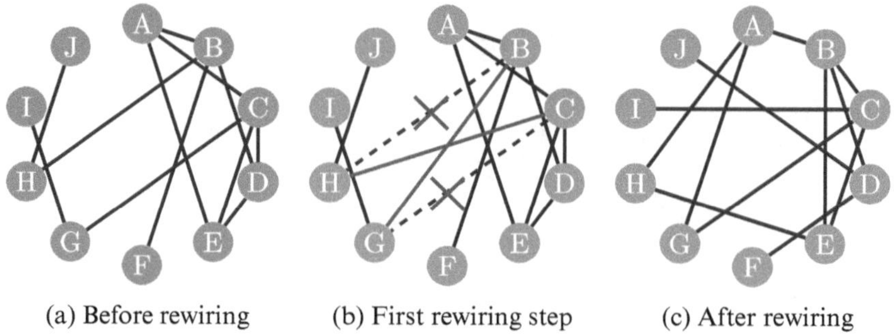

Figure 2.4 Rewiring example, applied to the 'core' network from Figure 2.3 (with nodes rearranged for ease of graphical representation)

prank phone calls tend to have a higher degree, and the density is the average number of calls made (or, equivalently, received) by each inhabitant during the week, divided by the number of inhabitants. Here, several network measures are quite meaningless: they might fluctuate from week to week, but only because of chance, not because they convey any information about the behavior of citizens. In particular, the clustering coefficient will typically be close to the density, assortativity will typically be close to zero, and average distance will depend on the density.[3] This is because if calls are made completely at random — as opposed to, say, specifically targeting friends or enemies — there is no actual social phenomenon to discover or analyze.

There is one aspect, though, under which this random, uninformative network is a very interesting tool for network scientists: as a *benchmark* for other network structures — those where clustering, assortativity and average distance provide meaningful information. Assume that researchers have data about calls occurring in the town, but they *ignore* whether inhabitants choose the phone numbers they call at random. Neither do they know if a specific rule is followed, but they *suspect* there is one and would like to have proof. In this case, they can *create* a fake network with the same distribution of degrees (reflecting the fact that some people like playing prank phone calls more than others) but with different edges, and compare this fake network to the original network.

The procedure by which the fake network is created is called *rewiring*. Take the original network (Figure 2.4a), pick any two edges not attached to the same node, and swap their endpoints, as in Figure 2.4b (if the network is undirected, we can indiscriminately designate any of the two nodes connected by each edge as its endpoint). Repeat this operation many times. The result (Figure 2.4c) will be a new network with different edges, but with the node degrees preserved. Regardless of this similarity, it will potentially have a very different 'shape' from the initial network. For instance, if the initial network is the one of friendship on Facebook, I will keep my number of friends unchanged, but I might have the same probability of being connected to people from my hometown, Perugia (Italy) and with people from Petropavlovsk-Kamcatskij, a similarly sized city in Kamcatka (Russia). If it is the network of US highways, Orlando will be connected with roughly the same probability to Tampa and to any other US city with as many highways as Tampa. Clearly, such a network will have lost a large part of its informative content. Moreover, as previously mentioned, most real world social and economic networks have positive clustering (friends of one's friends are often friends among themselves). Instead, in the rewired network, two friends of one person will have the same probability of being friends themselves as any two random individuals. In the end, this network will be pretty similar to the network of completely random phone calls.

The researchers studying the phenomenon of prank calls can hence compare a rewired network of calls — or even many different rewired networks — to the *true* network of calls. Do they have similar diameter, average distance, clustering coefficient, and assortativity? If the answer is 'yes', then it might be that this network really did not have anything interesting to reveal beyond the fact that 'some people play prank phone calls more than others', a statement that can be reached without any use of network theory. If the answer is instead 'no', then this can serve as the first step in the quest for understanding *how* citizens of this town actually pick their victims.

2.3 Networks are made of stars

In the previous chapter, a distinction was drawn between global measures — characterizing a network in its entirety — and local measures — characterizing a node and at most its immediate surroundings. However, we also saw that some measures, such as centrality, were somewhere in between these two extremes, as they focused on the position of a node *within* the entire network.

This distinction is important when analyzing a network from the point of view of contagion — an endeavor that can be tackled both at the aggregate level, by gauging the general susceptibility of the network to instances of contagion, or at the level of *a specific node*, or ensemble of nodes, trying to understand how it contributes to such susceptibility. This second approach will often involve some measure of centrality — as the guiding principle of centrality is really to capture how a node contributes to the 'connectedness' of a network.

The network of scientific collaboration (Figure 1.1p) is an interesting case study not just because it describes a fascinating phenomenon — the patterns of coauthorships characterizing the incessant advancement of science, all around the world — but also because we have complete and reliable data about it, provided by bibliographic databases. This is why we know for instance that it is a small world, as best exemplified by the Erdős number discussed in the previous chapter.

However, this 'smallness' does not derive from the fact that the typical researcher is similar to Erdős, frequently collaborating with a large number of colleagues from all parts of the world. Quite the opposite, the average researcher is relatively conservative in her choice of coauthors, often collaborating repeatedly with the same people, or maybe with coauthors of her former coauthors (say, members of their own department or research center). Put simply, researchers often exhibit strong clustering. However, collaboration habits are strongly heterogeneous, and *some* researchers compensate for the missing interconnectedness by taking a (literally) central role in the network (the Erdős number, after all, is not named after Erdős by coincidence). This was made evident in a study by researchers Sanjeev Goyal, Marco J. van der Leij, and José Luis Moraga-González, who examined the network of coauthorship among economists by analyzing articles published in a large number of scientific journals in the 1990s.[4] First, they observed that there was a *giant component* of authors — 40.7% of authors, to be exact — who are, in one way or another, connected to one another. Then, they observed that if they randomly removed 5% of the nodes (authors) from the network, not much would change: the giant component's size would decrease to just to 39.8% of active authors, and the clustering coefficient of the network would remain unchanged. But if instead they identified and removed from the network the 5% of *most connected* nodes, nicknamed 'stars' (a pun on the fact that these are typically important economists, and that the network around them looks like Figure 1.10b), then the giant component completely broke apart: the largest remaining component included only 0.1% of authors, and the clustering coefficient increased from 0.157 to 0.344.

Now assume we were to study the diffusion of a specific research practice that researchers learn from each other while collaborating. We may want to predict its speed of diffusion over the entire community *or* we could try to understand how a specific, very *central* researcher, contributes to it. We will see in the next chapters that both approaches are important in the study of instances of contagion relevant to the functioning and well-being of modern societies.

2.4 Robust networks

In general, is the presence of stars a *positive or negative* feature of a social or economic network? It can be both, since these are nodes that favor the spread of both positive and harmful types of contagion — which coexist, in many networks.

Since this book will mainly deal with negative types of contagion — just like public policies mostly deal with negative externalities — it could inadvertently give the impression that *connectivity is bad* in general, and that the nodes that vastly increase connectivity are specifically harmful, so that it would be in the public interest to limit, or somehow oppose, their very existence.

In fact, the positive role of connectedness in many networks is so evident as to be protected in various forms by governments — in networks as different as transportation, financial, communication. And ironically, stars are often seen as a *problem* not because they increase connectedness, but for the opposite reason: that removing them would cause a collapse of the network's connectedness, just like the network of coauthors becomes fragmented if we imagine suppressing the 5% most connected authors.

Consider the circle network and the star network (Figures 1.10a and 1.10b), and assume that they represent the shape of the railways networks in two different cities, or regions, with each node representing a station. Note that they have similar density — that is, similar number of connections: to be precise, a circle city with N stations is going to also have N connections, whereas a star city will have $N - 1$. They also have the same clustering coefficient, zero for both (neither contains any triangle). However, the similarities end here: they have different assortativity and, most importantly, different average distance and diameter, both being much smaller in the star (where no two stations are more than two 'hops' from each other) than in the circle city (where two opposite stations are $\frac{N}{2}$ or $\frac{N-1}{2}$ hops from each other depending on whether N is even or odd).

These differences seem to put the star network at a significant advantage, as lower distances are a benefit in transportation networks — they imply lower costs, lower commuting times, and hence less congestion ... However, what would happen to the network if we were to suddenly suppress a node — for instance because of an accident blocking transit through one of the stations? In the circle network, the answer is quickly given: it would transform into a line network. Distances would increase, in some cases dramatically (think about traveling from one to the other of the two stations previously neighboring the one that went out of service). In the star network, it clearly depends: if one of the peripheral stations was taken out of service, transports between the others would be virtually unaffected. If however the *central* station was taken out of service, it would block *all* transports in the city.

From this quick analysis, one could conclude that each city structure has its pros and cons: specifically, an accident in the circle city will always cause some moderate annoyance, while vice–versa, an accident in the star city will *tipically* have minimal consequences, but it might, with low probability, bring all transports to a halt. So if we had to say which of the two cities is more *resilient* to this kind of damage, the answer would probably be a matter of points of view (or more precisely, of *aversion to risk*).

This is true only to the extent that damage happens *randomly* to any given station. Things change drastically if we consider an *adversarial* attack on the two cities, that is, a hypothetical enemy or saboteur that acts with the precise aim of disrupting transport. In this eventuality, the circle pattern definitely has an advantage over the star pattern, where the attacker can, by appropriately directing their attack, paralyze the entire transportation network. By the way, even if we assume that damage is not adversarial — that is, it just happens as a consequence of usage, not of actual intention to cause damage — it is still likely that, in absence of specific precautions, the central station of the star city will be the one featuring more frequent failures, just because of its more intense use.

In fact, neither the circle nor the star network can be considered resilient networks: in the star, removing the central nodes is enough to completely break the network, but even in the circle it is enough to remove *two* nodes in order to break the network into two components, potentially reducing significantly the size of the largest single component. But this is unavoidable, given their very low density — $N - 1$ edges is the absolute minimum required to connect N nodes in a single component. In order to build more resilient networks, that can survive the removal of multiple nodes without breaking down into separate components, more edges are required. To take an extreme example, the complete network of Figure 1.10c will clearly survive the removal of multiple nodes or edges without breaking down — at the cost, however, of a very large number of edges, which are, in the case for instance of a railway network, obviously unaffordable for budget and practicality reasons.

2.5 A tale of two topologies

A stream of research has developed studying the *robustness*, or *resilience*, of different network structures to the removal of some of the network's nodes. A 2000 *Nature* study[5] has analyzed and compared two prototypical examples of networks — *topologies*, in the jargon of network theory. In both cases, the network had 10,000 nodes and 20,000 edges, but the procedure used to place the edges was very different between them: in one case it followed the so called *Erdős–Rényi* model,[6] in the other a *preferential attachment* model.

In the Erdős–Rényi model, edges are added one after the other (similar to the 'Edges in time' row of Figure 1.7) by each time randomly picking a pair of unconnected nodes and connecting them — 20,000 times. From this procedure, the researchers obtained a network where each node was on average connected to four other nodes (as each edge 'touches' two nodes), and most importantly, since all edges had the same probability of being created, nodes tended to have a degree *close* to four. Instead, in the preferential attachment model, nodes are added one at a time (similar to the row 'Nodes in time' of Figure 1.7), and each is attached to two other nodes, chosen among all pre–existing ones with a probability *proportional* to their degree. This is the essence of the *preferential* attachment: that new nodes attach to old ones in a way that is not purely random, but makes some nodes more and more 'popular' over time, ultimately resulting in a strong *heterogeneity* in the degree of nodes. Social scientists sometimes describe the mechanism as the 'Matthew effect', in reference to a sentence from the Gospel of Matthew stating '*to everyone who has, more shall be given*'.[7]

In the end, despite the two networks having the same number of edges (and nodes), they are very different in their structure. The difference can already be perceived by considering some standard network metrics: for instance, the network obtained with preferential attachment has lower diameter and average distance: 'popular' nodes, a bit like the center of the star network in Figure 1.10b, serve as hubs to connect and bring closer together parts of the network that would otherwise be remote from each other.

The distinction between the two topologies then becomes crucial when considering their robustness to the removal of nodes. Differently from the case of the circle and the star, both networks are sufficiently dense as to make them somewhat robust: specifically, they tend to have a 'giant component' comprising the vast majority of nodes, and that component will typically remain connected despite the removal of a few nodes. So an alternative way to measure 'resilience' is to compute how the removal of nodes affects the *diameter* of such a component — a network being less resilient if the diameter increases more when nodes are removed.

What we observe is that as long as we remove *randomly chosen* nodes, the network obtained by preferential attachment (also referred to in the literature as '*scale–free* network') is very robust, its diameter remaining roughly constant; the diameter of the network obtained with the Erdős–Rényi procedure instead progressively grows if we apply the same treatment. The reason is that in the scale–free network, connectivity is safe as long as the most important nodes are still there, and the most important nodes are few, so their suppression has low probability. But if, instead, the removal of nodes follows an *adversarial* approach, targeting the star nodes (in the case of the *Nature* study, those with highest degree), then the scale–free network is in trouble, as the diameter of the largest component grows steadily. Meanwhile, the Erdős–Rényi network is no more severely affected than with the suppression of random nodes — because again, most connected nodes in an Erdős–Rényi network are typically not *that much* more connected than random nodes.

It is not unusual for network scholars to create such large 'synthetic' networks according to specific rules, and then run simulations on them to understand how different phenomena — including node removal, different forms of contagion, and the like — will affect them. And the authors of the study just described did not chose the two specific topologies by chance. The Erdős–Rényi model essentially creates a network 'as random as possible'. Coming back to the town of prank phone calls, it is as if there was really *no rule* waiting to be brought to light by research, except for 'people sometimes play prank phone calls' (not even 'some people more than others'). The heterogeneity in the scale–free network, and the resulting *systemic* importance of few nodes, resembles instead what is observed in many real social and economic networks, where a few nodes are crucial for the entire network's connectivity: for instance, the authors of the *Nature* study analyze node removal also on the Internet, where each node is a server, and find that similar to the scale–free network, it is specifically vulnerable to *adversary* node removal.

While scholars may sometimes argue about whether a real world network is or is not 'scale–free',[8] it is uncontroversial that many important social and economic networks are more similar to the Internet network than to an Erdős–Rényi one — and that this has important consequences both when studying the robustness of the network to node removal, and its propensity to be a vehicle of contagion. In fact, the two things tend to go together, as we will see in the next chapters that those same nodes that provide connectivity to the network will also be crucial in spreading contagion. And more than 'should we favor or oppose stars?', the question will often be: 'since stars are there to stay, can we protect (the network from) them?'

2.6 Exploiting networks

Let us return for a moment to the case of a messaging app, such as WhatsApp. Assume that a marketing agent is trying to convince people who are not using this app to install it. He is well aware that every time he is able to recruit a new user, this in turn might push her friends to adopt the app too (as in Figure 2.2). So, in principle, he will want to target users who have many friends (for instance, he might pick his targets by looking at their lists of friends on Facebook). But he also knows that these friends might in turn push their friends to adopt the app: hence, he might prefer individuals *whose friends have many friends*, whose friends' friends have many friends, and so on.

So how could the agent rank subjects based on *how well connected they are* — that is, taking into account their number of friends, but also of their friends' friends, and so on? Questions such as this emerge from a multiplicity of different contexts involving networks, and the answer lies most often in (one of the forms of) *centrality*. The agent will not find an answer by just looking at node degrees — or a rewired network.

In essence, one could state that the main difference between the traditional approach to externalities and the 'network science' approach is the difference between the degree of a node and its centrality. It is both a conceptual and an operational difference. Conceptual because it reminds us that if we are part of a large network, focusing only on our immediate neighborhood gives us a restricted view of how our actions influence other people, and how other people's actions influence us. Operational because it implies a constant urge to collect network data and use it as a basis for decision making. Today, networks are more important than even a couple of decades ago both not only in the sense that we *are* more interconnected, but also in the sense that we have more information about our connections. The first aspect means we have more things to take into consideration, and the second means we have the *responsibility* to take them into consideration — in no small part because malicious individuals may make destructive use of this information.

Our marketing agent has far more powerful tools at his disposal than a decade ago to identify the target subjects of his campaign. Policymakers have new tools, too, and also must use them. Tools such as centrality measures allow citizens and governments to extract *intelligible meaning* from networks that are *complex*. A complex system is any system in which many parts interact, to the point that its behavior cannot be easily predicted by studying the behavior of individual parts, taken in isolation. Note that a complex system is something very different from a *complicated* system. The tax system in many countries is *complicated*: the large number of laws, rules, and specific cases to consider might intimidate non–specialists (and in some cases, specialists, too). Instead, the basic ingredients for a snow avalanche are simple: tiny droplets of frozen water. But this does not mean that it is easy for physicists to predict avalanches. Scientists say that a system is complex when its ingredients are relatively simple, but it features characteristics or behaviors that would have hardly been imaginable given only those ingredients.

Societies, markets, and online social networks are all examples of human environments featuring complex dynamics: for instance, the dynamics of a stock market crash are often compared to those of an avalanche. And the complexity of some human systems is such that even the metaphor of an avalanche does not do them justice. It might be tempting to compare revolutions to avalanches, each rebel providing momentum to — and gaining momentum from — other rebels, turning a potentially irrelevant puff of discontent into an unstoppable movement. But the iconic image of the 'Tank Man', confronting a column of tanks in Tiananmen Square on June 5, 1989, or the 'I have a dream' speech given by Martin Luther King Jr. on August 28, 1963, are *symbols* of dignity that cannot be rivaled by even the most energetic snowflake. A particle can push another particle in a domino effect, but it cannot represent a *model* for other particles to follow or avoid.

The theory of complex systems often goes hand in hand with the theory of networks; and rightly so, because many real–world networks are complex, and many complex systems can be represented as networks. But it is important to understand where the similarity ends. The theory of complexity can help establish the probability of avalanches. In some cases, it can have immediate applications — for instance, advising skiers to not venture on a given slope on a given day with specific climatic conditions. But it will not help identify *the* snowflake that will drive the next avalanche, simply because there is no such thing as an 'intrinsic propensity to avalanches' for snowflakes: the danger of avalanches can only come from large masses of snow. Instead, the toolkit of the theory of networks includes measures that characterize *individual* nodes and edges, and that can be interpreted as the risk of contagion, or the intensity of an externality, all the while *taking into account* their position in the network. Analyzing a network locally, node by node, is also a prerequisite for *acting on it* locally. The failure of that small–town bank may not drive the collapse of the global financial system, but if the analysis of its financial relationships can help save it from bankruptcy, it is still worth doing.

Network theory in its more successful applications is simply the art of examining individual parts in their context.

Notes

1 Coase, 1960.

2 Persky, 1995.

3 For towns with a large number of inhabitants, the average distance will be close to $\frac{\log n}{\log d}$, where n is the number of nodes and d the average degree (A. Fronczak, P. Fronczak, and Hołyst, 2004).

4 Goyal, Van Der Leij, and Moraga-González, 2006.
5 Albert, Jeong, and Barabási, 2000.
6 Yes, this is the same Erdős from which the Erdős number is named.
7 Merton, 1968.
8 Broido and Clauset, 2019; Voitalov et al., 2019.

Bibliography

Albert, Réka, Hawoong Jeong, and Albert-László Barabási (2000). 'Error and attack tolerance of complex networks'. In: *Nature* 406.6794, pp. 378–382.

Broido, Anna D and Aaron Clauset (2019). 'Scale-free networks are rare'. In: *Nature Communications* 10.1, p. 1017.

Coase, Ronald H (1960). 'The problem of social cost'. In: *Classic Papers in Natural Resource Economics*. Springer, pp. 87–137.

Fronczak, Agata, Piotr Fronczak, and Janusz A Hołyst (2004). 'Average path length in random networks'. In: *Physical Review E* 70.5, p. 056110.

Goyal, Sanjeev, Marco J Van Der Leij, and José Luis Moraga-González (2006). 'Economics: An emerging small world'. In: *Journal of Political Economy* 114.2, pp. 403–412.

Merton, Robert K (1968). 'The Matthew effect in science: The reward and communication systems of science are considered'. In: *Science* 159.3810, pp. 56–63.

Persky, Joseph (1995). 'The ethology of Homo Economicus'. In: *Journal of Economic Perspectives* 9.2, pp. 221–231.

Voitalov, Ivan et al. (2019). 'Scale-free networks well done'. In: *Physical Review Research* 1.3, p. 033034.

3 Epidemics and networks

The Betrothed ('I Promessi Sposi'), a cornerstone of Italian literature, includes a detailed, if romanticized, account of the plague epidemic that devastated Milan in 1630, killing around 60,000 people out of a population of 130,000 — admittedly small numbers compared to the 'Black Death' plague pandemic that had killed at least 75 million people in Europe a couple of centuries before (close to 50% of the populations involved), but still corresponding to half of the population, an enormous share even when compared to COVID–19.

The chronicle, based on sources contemporaneous to the event, begins with a description of how the contagion reached Milan, coming from certain villages in the northern part of the province. It describes the slow, and inadequate, response both of the authorities, initially unconvinced about the identification of the disease, and of the population, which joked lightheartedly at the first news of the epidemic. Things did not improve when the population started to take it seriously: the mass of people that gathered in a procession on June 11, 1630, to ask for divine help against the disease actually gave it a strong boost. Manzoni's account then depicts several of the social and economic aspects of the tragedy (*'The frenzy had propagated like the contagion'*), which form the background to the vicissitudes of Renzo, the main character from the book. He is able to easily enter the city, despite the prohibition imposed by the authorities, but then later he is almost killed by a crowd of residents who consider him a *poisoner*, that is, an individual devoted to intentionally spreading the plague, through the use of some mysterious powder, or liquid. Indeed, it is a historical fact that innocent people were executed because they were suspected of being poisoners, often falsely admitting their own guilt after days of relentless torture. In fact, in another writing, 'History of the Infamous Column', Manzoni discusses the fate of one of these innocent victims, Gian Giacomo Mora, today remembered by a plaque on a street bearing his name, in the center of Milan.

Medicine has made enormous leaps forward since 1630, and today antibiotic treatments are typically successful in healing individuals who contract plague, if diagnosed early.[1] But the most effective instrument for fighting the disease, and reducing its death toll, remains the isolation of infected subjects: a 'technology' that was, in principle, just as available in 1630 (like several other cities,

DOI: 10.4324/9781003490951-3

Milan had its own lazaretto, or quarantine station, managed by Capuchin friars rather than civil authorities) as it is today. However, isolation of infected subjects requires information on them; and our ability to gather and process information *has* changed in the last four centuries.

In 1630, the first infected person who brought the plague to Milan was able (just like Renzo) to enter the city and spread the epidemic; today, instead, even with 10–15 cases occurring in the United States annually, the last person–to–person contagion was reported in 1925. Once a diagnosis for plague is made, strict hygienic precautions are taken: in particular, the infected individual is put in respiratory isolation. And while the World Health Organization does not recommend vaccination ('except for high–risk groups'), it does provide a detailed list of instructions mostly focused on hygiene and isolation.

In countries where health interventions are less prompt, the plague is still a relevant threat, causing the death of 584 people worldwide between 2010 and 2015, and 202 in Madagascar in 2017 only. In 1994, 57 people died from an outbreak in Surat, India, and 300,000 left the city *out of fear that it would be quarantined,*[2] — thereby actively thwarting prevention measures.

If isolation, quarantines, and monitoring are powerful weapons in the war against the plague — a disease which we can treat with antibiotics — they play an even more critical role in the fight against other transmissible diseases for which we still have *no definitive cure*. This was the case of COVID–19, the coronavirus that starting in December 2019 from the Chinese city of Wuhan, caused the fifth deadliest epidemic in history. Commenting on the outbreak, C. Raina MacIntyre, a professor of biosecurity at the University of New South Wales, stated, 'We learnt that epidemics can be controlled without drugs or vaccines, using enhanced surveillance, case isolation, contact tracking, PPE [Personal Protective Equipment] and infection control measures'.[3] This statement might seem bold in retrospect, but it is an honest description of what can (or *could*) be done.

In the COVID–19 epidemic, all of the strategies mentioned by Prof. MacIntyre have been employed, with entire cities halted, people locked in their apartments, cruise ships quarantined. But commentators have related the impressive spread of the outbreak to the ambiguous attitude of Chinese authorities during the first phases, when doctors who tried to raise alarm about the risk of contagion were reprimanded.[4] And even though many countries, starting with Italy in February 2020, were hit hard by the epidemic despite having a relatively modern health system and more time to prepare countermeasures (and no systematic attempt to suppress freedom of speech), it is at least plausible that the initial hesitancy by Chinese authorities was determinant in transforming the epidemic in a global catastrophe.

To get an idea of what the reconstruction of the initial steps of the pandemic could have been, it is interesting to retrace the beginning of another pandemic which had, some time before, conquered the public opinion's attention, and against which there was no cure: the Ebola outbreak that hit Western

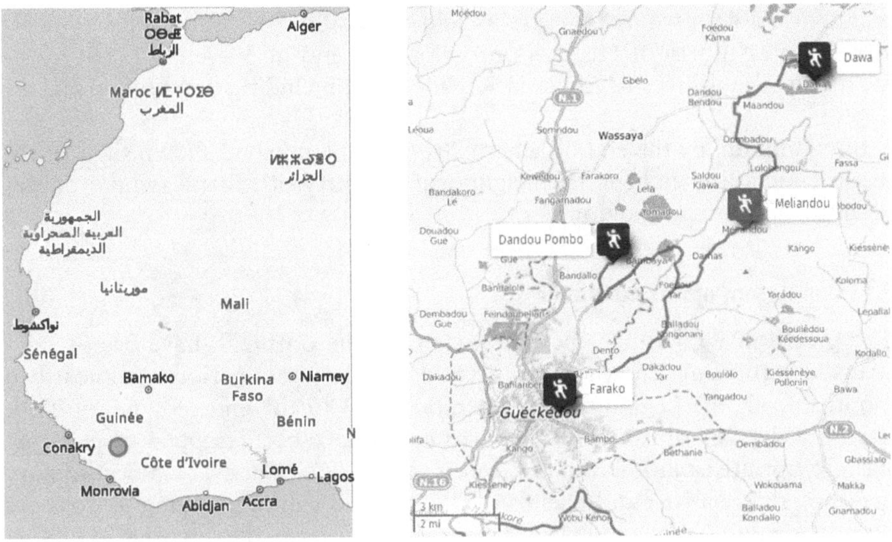

Figure 3.1 Map of the region from where the 2013 Ebola outbreak originated

Africa between 2013 and 2016, causing more than 11,000 deaths and enormous economic losses in the region.

A group of researchers from France, Germany, and Guinea, in an article published in the New England Journal of Medicine,[5] reconstructed the first steps of the contagion, concluding that the 'index case' (first infected human) of the outbreak was a 2-year-old boy who might have caught the disease from a colony of fruit bats living near his village, Meliandou, in the Guéckédou prefecture of Guinea. The child exhibited the first symptoms on December 2, 2013, and he died within four days. But prior to his death, he had transmitted the disease to his sister, mother, grandmother, to a nurse and to a 'village midwife', all of whom would die within a couple of months. The virus then traveled to the nearby village of Dandou Pombo in the body of a family member of the midwife, who had taken care of her sick relative. In the meanwhile, at the boy's grandmother's funeral, two other people from the near village of Dawa also contracted the virus, which they passed on to three other inhabitants of the village. By the end of January 2014, almost two months after the index case, the Ebola outbreak had taken the lives of 10–15 people in a handful of villages within a 15-kilometer radius (Figure 3.1).

Meanwhile, the sick midwife was hospitalized in Guéckédou, the namesake town of the district with a population of approximately 200,000 residents. She arrived there on January 25, and died on February 2, but not before she transmitted the virus to a nurse who attended to her. In turn, the nurse was hospitalized in Macenta, a city 60 kilometers from Guéckédou, where he died on February 10. In the Macenta hospital, 15 people died over the next few weeks, including a doctor whose funeral was held in Kissidougou, a city approximately 70 kilometers north of Guéckédou. Before the end of March 2014, five people had lost their lives to Ebola in Kissidougou, including two brothers of the doctor.

Summing up, by the end of March 2014, 130 people had shown signs of the disease, including eight in the neighboring country of Liberia (whose border lies just south of Guéckédou).

3.1 Contagion, out of metaphor

The precision with which the initial steps of the outbreak have been reconstructed is thrilling. In hindsight, it is clear there was a period of almost two months, from the beginning of December 2013 to the end of January 2014, during which the diffusion of the virus could have been stopped by ensuring the appropriate isolation of a few dozen people (including, as a precautionary measure, the relatives and friends of the infected subjects), living in no more than four small Guinean villages. However, at the time, the disease had not yet been identified as Ebola, and clearly infected subjects were not being identified or tracked. As a result, the outbreak raged on until it was finally defeated on January 14, 2016, more than two years and 11,000 deaths later, and even then its defeat was only possible after a massive international effort and at enormous economic costs to all Western Africa.

Even though we likely will never know it with such level of detail, also in the case of COVID–19 there was some time where stopping the diffusion of the virus would have avoided millions of deaths at a very low cost. In retrospect, it is easy to identify what 'should have been done'; but the account of the first weeks of the Ebola outbreak is impressive, and informative, because it reveals how — similar to the case of the plague in *The Betrothed* — *information* and *organization*, more than cures or vaccines, were the missing 'technologies' that could have changed the course of events. This includes not just the actual identification of the disease as Ebola (the first medical investigators presumed they were facing a strand of the much more diffused — but easier to cure — cholera), but also information about movements of infected individuals. In the same way, COVID–19 was initially mistaken for pneumonia, and later studies have shown that when the first cases were identified, the virus had been circulating for weeks, or even months.[6]

Summing up, information about networks over which infective diseases spread is paramount. And in many ways, some aspects of the accounts of the outbreak's first steps bring to mind the 'network view of the world' discussed in the previous chapters. In the very first days of the contagion, subjects contracted Ebola at a *funeral* on two occasions; on two other occasions, it happened in a *hospital* (a hospital, in Alzano Lombardo, was also crucial in transforming the province of Bergamo, and Italy in general, into one of the regions most severely hit by the pandemic globally between February and March 2020). These 'coincidences' are hardly surprising considering the Ebola virus can spread by contact with an infected subject's bodily fluids, including broken skin.[7] This means that the social network over which the virus travels strongly depends on physical contact among subjects. Gather a sizable number of people around the body of an Ebola patient, deceased or alive, and the number of edges in the network suddenly increases – and with it, the probability of contagion (it is not a coincidence that the words 'contact' and 'contagion' come from the same Latin verb *tago*, that means 'to touch').

Funerals and hospitals share another feature (in particular in regions of the world where hospitals are dispersed, and of variable quality): people travel long distances to reach them. This is a crucial — and unfortunate, in the case of Ebola — feature for the simple reason that normally, people tend to interact with other people in their proximity. If each villager only interacted with fellow villagers — that is, if the network of social interaction was composed of perfectly isolated clusters, as in Figure 1.10d — then there would be no way for a virus such as Ebola to reach outside the village of the index case. But modern societies are not composed of isolated villages, and this represents a weakness that will only intensify over time: there is a reason if the Western African Ebola epidemic was the most lethal Ebola outbreak in the history of humanity, and the COVID–19 outbreak has reached all of the world with a speed that is unrivaled by large epidemics in history. Indeed, mobility is much more accessible today than in past centuries, and the share of individuals living in urban areas, high populated, is much larger even compared to just few decades ago.

A joint research group from Italy and the US has estimated that, concerning the Ebola outbreak, 'up to Aug 16, 2014 [...] 38.3% of infections [...] were acquired in hospitals, [...] 8.6% [...] while participating in funerals'.[8] Another context in which a virus can easily spread, because of a large gathering of people, is a market: and indeed, the Huanan Seafood Wholesale Market in Wuhan has borne an important role in the 2019 COVID–19 outbreak.[9] Incidentally, funerals, hospitals and markets are all contexts which authorities can monitor with relative ease — more than the ordinary life of each Guinean villager, at least.

3.2 Epidemiological stars

The sister, mother, grandmother and nurse of the index case for the Ebola outbreak were infected and then died, but they apparently did not transmit the disease to anybody else. Instead it was the midwife who was the first to carry the virus to a larger town when she was hospitalized in Guéckédou, and the nurse who contracted Ebola in Guéckédou gave the outbreak a boost by traveling to Macenta and spreading the infection there.

According to Western media outlets, it was the long incubation period in the remote and isolated villages of Western Africa, with limited or no access to formal health care, that delayed the humanitarian effort for weeks, resulting in thousands of deaths. But the ironic truth is that relatively few people were infected in such villages and it was ultimately the health care infrastructure that played such a fundamental role in the spread of the disease: in 2014 in Africa just like in 2020 in Northern Italy. Ironic, but not surprising: a health care worker has both a much larger indegree (probability of catching the virus) and a much larger outdegree (probability of transmitting the virus, once infected) than an ordinary subject — unless particular measures against infection are taken, of course. Indeed, understanding the features of social networks (the network of physical interaction, in this case) is a critical instrument in predicting the diffusion of an epidemic and enacting protective countermeasures.

As mentioned in Chapter 1, most social networks exhibit high levels of clustering, and the networks over which Ebola, COVID–19 and other diseases spread are no exception: villagers often interact with other villagers. However, we also know that social networks are often 'small worlds' in the sense that no two nodes of the network are very far apart (or, in other words, that the diameter is smaller than one might expect from a strongly clustered network). These two properties seem to oppose one another: one suggesting that people form small, isolated communities (as in Figure 1.10d) and the other suggesting that no two people are that distant from each other (as in Figure 1.10c). Indeed, the key is in the star nodes discussed in the previous chapter, that vastly reduce the diameter and the average distance of networks — and hence the time needed for the contagion to spread.

Many social networks have stars, and again, the networks over which Ebola, COVID–19 and other diseases spread are no exception. The thought experiment of removing well connected nodes from a scale–free network is akin to that of removing the nurse, the midwife, the doctor, and other 'star individuals' from the social network from which Ebola started, or removing the Wuhan market, the hospital in Alzano Lombardo and some crowded public transports from the social network over which COVID–19 spread. We would be left with a large number of small, isolated components — such as families and villages — each exhibiting high clustering — that is, whose members mostly know and hang out with each other. In such a social network, the potential for the spread of COVID–19 would have been quite limited.

Unless specific precautions are taken (in the later stages of the Ebola epidemic, Western media outlets were full of pictures of workers in eye-catching safety suits, providing protection from infected patients), health workers such as the nurse will be the star nodes in the network, and it is only natural that they will play a crucial role in the spread of the epidemic.

Obviously, the kind of individual that is a star in the network of epidemiological diffusion depends on the type of disease. For Ebola, contagion requires some form of physical contact, while for COVID–19, which is airborne, anybody who attended crowded places without sufficient precautions could be a vector. Indeed, if a number of people meet in a crowded room without face masks or appropriate ventilation, it is as if a *complete* network (Figure 1.10c) formed. It is not by chance that a crucial figure in the diffusion of COVID–19 was represented by so called *superspreaders* — positive individuals who transmit the disease to a large number of other individuals — and by *superspreading events* — occasions, such as weddings, ceremonies or even choir rehearsal — to which a relevant number of new cases is attributed.

3.3 Reconstructing networks

In the previous chapter, stars where initially described with reference to the coauthorship network, where it is not difficult to identify them, because conveniently, all the information required is stored in a single digital archive. But for epidemiological researchers and health officials, such precise mapping is not possible due to a lack of complete and reliable descriptions about the social networks over which epidemics spread. And there are very good reasons for this, aside from technical limitations: unlike a scientific publication, which is by definition public, databases recording with precision each interpersonal interaction — from casual chatting to sexual intercourse — of any citizen of a country would pose privacy issues that make even the most authoritarian regimes of the planet pale in comparison.

So apart from the different types of connections and of possible contagion, one important difference between the network of scientific coauthorship and that of physical interaction is the degree to which researchers are able to observe them. In fact, even the laborious reconstruction of the initial Ebola outbreak is incomplete in this sense, because it only includes actual infections, and not contacts that did not result in contagion. In the same way, while an article published in the *American Journal of Medicine* in 1984[10] made news by allegedly tracing the diffusion of HIV in the USA to a so called 'patient zero' — a Canadian flight attendant at the center of an intricate web of sexual relations — this was refuted by a 2016 article,[11] and today the origins of the HIV epidemic in the United States are considered unknown.

Today epidemiologists typically understand how, mechanically, a virus spreads from human to human; they know that some individuals have a much higher propensity to catch and spread the disease, and they know that this propensity depends not just on physiological characteristics and environmental factors, but also on the position in the social network of the physical interaction. But they also know that precisely analyzing such a network in real time is just not possible. So what is the role for network theory if the network in question is extremely important but *unknown*? The answer to this question requires an understanding of which *features* of the network are most important in order to study and predict the diffusion of epidemics, and the first obvious feature is the *density*, or (equivalently) the average degree.

To make the point, consider a world in which, like Jim Carrey in the movie *Truman Show*, everyone meets with exactly the same people every day — that is, such that the social network under analysis does not change over time — and consider a virus which, whenever an infected subject meets a healthy subject, has a probability of $\frac{1}{2}$ of infecting the healthy subject.

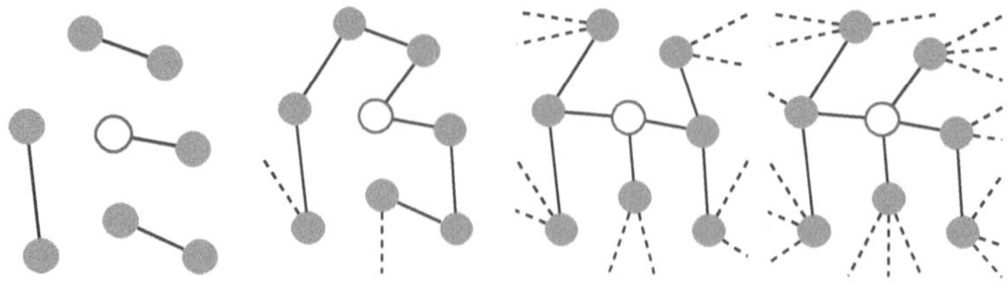

Figure 3.2 Examples of fixed–degree networks

How quickly will the virus spread if the degree of each node in the network is one (that is, each person is only in contact with one other person)? A network in which the degree of each node is one can only be composed of many pairs of subjects connected among them, as in Figure 3.2a. Consider a sexually transmitted infection in a society where all individuals are perpetually monogamous (and faithful). Either the infected subject will pass the disease to the partner (two infected subjects in total) or not (one infected subject in total); in any either case, the disease will not spread further.

To make things more interesting — and realistic — we must consider a society with more connections. What if, for instance, nodes have a degree of two rather than one? A network in which each subject is in contact with two other people every day will take the form of a collection of circles (as in Figure 3.2b). The index subject can now have two neighbors, and he will *probably* transmit the disease to at least one of them (there is only one probability out of four that he does not). And if a neighbor is unlucky enough to catch the disease, she has a probability of $\frac{1}{2}$ of infecting her *other* neighbor, who, if infected, will in turn have a probability of $\frac{1}{2}$ of spreading the disease, and so on. At each step of this epidemic, establishing whether or not the disease will spread further is equivalent to tossing a coin: whenever the coin lands on heads, the epidemic stops. Clearly, the coin will not land on tails forever — that is, we can expect the disease to spontaneously stop at some point.

To make things even worse, consider a network in which the degree of each node is three. Such a network is less trivial to analyze because it can take much more complex forms than just circles. Still, with the exception of the index case — who has three neighbors — each infected individual will have at most two neighbors to possibly infect (that is, *healthy* neighbors), as in Figure 3.2c. In other words, at each step of contagion, the number of possible infections doubles. At the same time, we know that the probability of each contact causing an infection is $\frac{1}{2}$: that is, on average, each infected subject passes the disease to *one* of her healthy neighbors.[12] Intuitively, the population and the disease are playing a 'fair game' at each step, where each of the two players can win with a probability of $\frac{1}{4}$ (the probability that both, or none, of the two healthy neighbors are infected), tie with a probability of $\frac{1}{2}$ (the probability that one of the two healthy neighbors is infected), or lose with the probability $\frac{1}{4}$. The winner of this fair game is given by an elementary statistical result known as the name of 'gambler's ruin'. The propagation of the disease is comparable to a casino that offers a coin–tossing game, where both the gambler and the croupier bet $1, and the coin determines who wins. At each round, the gambler and the croupier have exactly the same probability of winning, but the gambler has a limited budget, so if he plays forever, sooner or later he will go bankrupt, and the game will end there. A similar fate awaits our 'degree three epidemics': many people can possibly be infected, but in a large enough social network, eventually the outbreak is expected to extinguish spontaneously, leaving the vast majority unaffected.

Once more, let us make this disease more dangerous by increasing the degree of each node to four, as in the example of Figure 3.2d. And once more, let us assume that some neighbor of our index case is infected. This time, the probability that none of his other healthy neighbors becomes infected ($\frac{1}{8}$) is much lower than the probability that at least two do become infected ($\frac{1}{2}$). In fact, each infected subject will infect 1.5 healthy neighbors on average. Hence, we can expect the disease to grow over time not only in the sense that more people are infected over time, but also that *each day*, there are more newly infected subjects (50% more) than on the previous day.[13] This disease will now follow an *exponential* growth pattern: this term, often used metaphorically in common speech, applies here literally. In an exponentially growing epidemic, the *total* number of infected subjects increases by a given percentage every day.[14]

If we consider a network with even larger degree, the same exercise will result in an exponential growth with a larger daily percentage increase of cases. Such examples, while simplified, reveal the importance of identifying the characteristics of a social network not just to describe the network itself — connections of some kind between individuals — but also phenomena taking place *over* the network — contagion. Still, it is worth spending a couple of words on the main characteristics of an infective disease that these examples do *not* feature. Firstly: not all subjects in a given society will have the same number of connections, and as already mentioned, this heterogeneity is important in the diffusion of a disease. Secondly: we imagined that the neighbors of an infected subject — apart from the one the subject got the infection from — are sane: in reality, they might have already caught the disease from other contacts. Thirdly: we are considering a disease where diffusion essentially depends from one–to–one contacts. Many diseases, including COVID–19, often spread in contexts where *many people* meet. Fourthly: modern societies are clearly different from *Truman Show*, and in practice we meet different people every day. Fifthly: beyond healing time from the disease, another important factor to determine its dangerousness is incubation time, that is, how much time after having contracted the infection a subject will in turn be infective.

Despite all these limits, the examples we have seen cleanly feature two characteristics of the initial phase of diffusion of infective diseases: exponential growth, and the fact that the rate of growth depends on the density of the

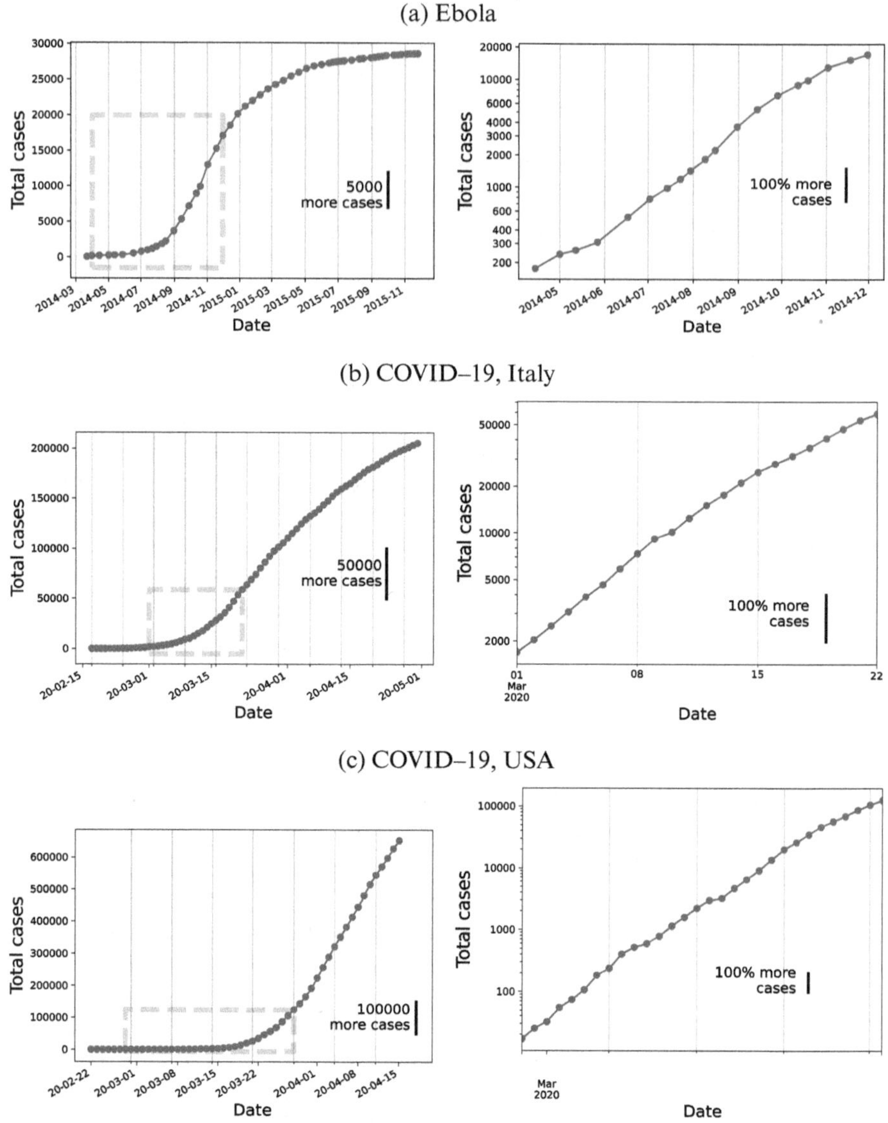

Figure 3.3 Growth of positive cases in the early phase of epidemics

network of contact. The one described above is just the simplest possible *compartimental* model, where a given population is split in 'compartments' — those who have not caught the disease, those who are currently sick, those who have recovered … — with rules determining how many people transition from one compartment to another over time. In the last decades, a rich stream of research has studied such compartimental models over networks of many different kinds,[15] enriching them with many of the aspects that the oversimplified model above purposely ignores.

Every epidemic that the human population deals with reminds the public opinion — not just researchers — that data is key; and the first data item that news outlets tend to focus on is the count of positive cases, together with its variation over time. This data is often to be considered incomplete (and this was definitely the case both for Ebola and for COVID–19), but despite this, data remains of fundamental importance to get a sense of how the diseases progress. The left side of Figure 3.3 displays the growth of cases of Ebola in 2014–2015 in the world, and of COVID–19 in 2020 respectively in Italy (the first European country to be severely hit) and in the USA (the country that ultimately reported the most fatalities). On the right, instead, we see the same data but zooming in on the dashed rectangle, and represented with a *logarithmic* scale, that emphasizes *percentage* growth. Hence, vertical distance between two points on the right does not indicate (as it does in the figures on the left) an increase by a given *number of cases*, but by a given *percentage* of cases. We can for instance verify that in the bottom left plot, the distance between 100 and 1,000 is the same as between 1,000 and 10,000, in both cases corresponding to an increase of 1,000%. On this scale, the spread of the epidemic over the time periods considered roughly follows a straight line, that researchers immediately recognize as a trademark of exponential growth.

Hence, these figures show that over such periods of time, the number of positive cases roughly increased by the same *percentage* every day. For the records, this percentage is more or less 2% for Ebola, and 18.4% and 35.9% for COVID–19 in Italy and in the United States, respectively. That this rule of 'constant percentage growth' also applies to the simple examples above is not a coincidence, but rather signals that, despite their simplicity, these thought experiments are capturing the primary mechanism behind contagion. Indeed, during the years of the pandemic, citizens of countries all around the world have sadly learned to recognize the exponential curves that describe the case count of COVID–19 among their fellow citizens.

In fact, epidemiologists identify the potential threat of an infectious disease first and foremost with its *basic reproduction number*, also known as R_0, which is simply defined as the average number of transmissions from an infected subject in an otherwise healthy population. In other words, susceptibility to a disease is really a characteristic of a *society*, not just of a virus, and R_0 indicates how easily a disease will spread within a given population. In the examples above, this threshold depends solely on the disease-specific probability of infection over an existing link — which was set to $\frac{1}{2}$ for simplicity — and the degree of nodes; in practice, susceptibility to an infection will change from social group to social group, from health system to health system, from season to season, and even according to changes in behavior of a same populations.[16] Hence, the basic reproduction number summarizes many factors in the society and of its environment in a single, yet important, figure.

There is a direct, and relatively simple, relationship between the basic reproduction number of an infectious disease and the share of population that must be vaccinated in order to guarantee herd immunity (or HIT, standing for 'herd immunity threshold'). For instance measles is a very contagious disease with a basic reproduction number that is typically assumed to lie between 12 and 18, depending on the context[17] (compared to 1.5–2.5 for Ebola,[18] and 2.4–4.1 for SARS-CoV-2[19]). This results in an HIT between 92% and 95%: if less than 92% of individuals are vaccinated, the population is in danger, particularly so immunodeficient members of the population (for COVID–19, this threshold has been calculated at around 70%, but the estimate was then corrected upwards as new variants appeared).

These numbers serve as a reminder that no–vax campaigns put at risk not just those who refrain from vaccinating themselves or their offspring, but their entire society — in particular individuals that because of other medical conditions cannot get vaccinated. While measles may no longer be considered a major health issue in developed countries, it is unfortunately making a comeback in the United States and Europe due to a fraudulent paper published in 1998 on The Lancet, a leading medical journal. The article cited false claims of links between vaccines and autism, causing a large number of families to not vaccinate their kids, resulting in new measles outbreaks, which claimed 81 lives in Europe between 2017 and 2019.[20] Interestingly, the COVID–19 pandemic has drastically lowered the number of cases of measles in Europe: the 127 cases recorded in 2022 represent a 99% decrease compared to 2018 and 96% compared to 2019: it is highly likely that control measures implemented against COVID–19 contributed to this (although some underreporting cannot be ruled out).[21]

3.4 Beyond the average degree

The average degree of nodes in a social network can reveal a lot about epidemiological risk in a society but more sophisticated measures can extract even more information from social networks, which can be useful in the study of epidemics.

Nodes — individuals — differ among themselves, including in the way in which they are interconnected, and these differences play a critical role in the diffusion of epidemics. For instance, toddlers who stay at home are a much less dangerous vehicle for the spread of diseases than health workers. But in order to exploit this awareness, and the tools for measuring networks, we must have data describing the network — that is, observe physical social interactions.

In fact, researchers began to realize the importance of social networks for understanding epidemics long before they had access to actual network data. In 1991, the epidemiologists Roy Anderson and Robert May proposed the concept of the 'who acquires infection from whom' table — or the *WAIFW matrix*.[22] This powerful instrument stems from a simple intuition: in reality, the probability of infection between any two subjects can differ greatly depending on the

Table 3.1 Hypothetical WAIFW matrix for an airborne disease

		Age of potential transmitter			
		0–5	**6–20**	**21–75**	**>75**
Age of potential receiver	**0–5**	low	low	medium	very low
	6–20	low	high	medium	low
	21–75	medium	medium	medium	low
	>75	low	medium	low	medium

circumstances. For instance, if the two subjects never meet, the probability of infection is zero; if instead they live in the same house, the probability might be quite high. Ideally, researchers would like to know the probability of infection between any two individuals but this is impossible. Hence, they attempt to characterize the probability of infection between *categories* of subjects.

Again, toddlers who stay home are examples of relatively low-risk individuals. But there is an abrupt change when they start attending school; as any parent knows, the probability that they contract an illness skyrockets then, and with it, the probability that their parents also contract it. Moreover, given that an adolescent in school will interact every day, for several hours, with several other adolescents, the probability that he contracts an illness *from another classmate* is much higher than the probability that he contracts an illness from, say, a toddler or an elderly person. Similarly, the probability that an adult contracts an illness from a toddler is different from the probability that an adult contracts an illness from an adolescent.

This is the essence of the WAIFW matrix: it can be still seen as a network, however it only approximates the actual social network of contact, by identifying nodes with *groups* of individuals. One example of the WAIFW matrix is shown in Table 3.1. Although simple, it conveys some important information: that individuals tend to interact with — and hence contract an illness from — people in their same age group, but also that toddlers are an exception, because they tend to mostly interact with older people, and that older people are more susceptible to illness, hence a grandfather has a higher probability of catching the disease from an adolescent grandchild than vice versa. The same example is visualized in its network form in Figure 3.4. One particular aspect of such a weighted network is that there are also edges from one node to itself — that is, from subjects of a given age group to subjects of the same age group. This is something we might not typically find in networks where each node corresponds to a subject (a subject will not *infect herself*).

Importantly, this kind of structure allows for not only the study the disease, but also the shaping of interventions. For instance, it tells us that if a compulsory vaccine is introduced for infants, the initial benefit in terms of spillover to the entire population might be limited for the first few years, but it will become substantial once the immunized children begin attending school. In contrast

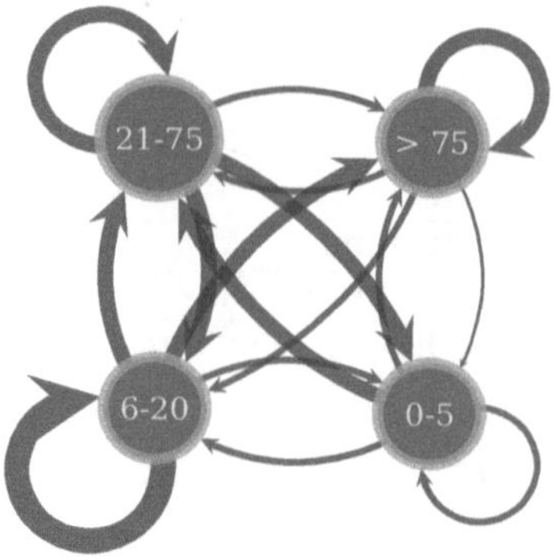

Figure 3.4 Weighted network corresponding to Table 3.1

to the example in Table 3.1, a real WAIFW matrix will contain actual numbers, and when researchers are considering a given intervention, it simulates the intervention's effectiveness with higher precision than solely considering the average probability of contagion. Recall that the description of the PageRank algorithm in Chapter 1 was based on the intuition of a web surfer who clicks on random links for a long period of time. Contagion can be similarly simulated by imagining a virus strain that randomly follows edges in Figure 3.4 and that follows larger edges with higher probability.

WAIFW matrices can be made more precise — and complex — by increasing the number of categories: for instance, they can consider narrower age intervals and/or other characteristics such as gender, so that one category might be 'women age 31', and one cell might represent the probability of a woman aged 31 contracting the disease from a child aged 2. But there is still the question of how to actually construct a WAIFW matrix since it summarizes the shape of a network we do not have access to. After all, the WAIFW matrix in Table 3.1 is reasonable, but in the end merely the result of guesswork.

The intuition of May and Anderson was to reconstruct the matrix from actual epidemiological data — although of a non–network nature. Health officials and researchers typically know the age of infected patients (see, for instance, Figure 3.5 for the weekly age distribution of cases of COVID–19 in USA from March to November 2022), and such data allow them to infer, with appropriate mathematical techniques, the values in the WAIFW matrix.[23]

One important limit of WAIFW matrices, then, is that they are contingent on the availability of abundant, and reasonably precise, data from actual diseases contracted *in the population of interest*. Data on the diffusion of COVID–19 in Italy may not tell us much on its diffusion in the US, and a WAIFW matrix for Ebola (which mostly transmits via contact) might not tell us much about COVID–19. What does the WAIFW matrix for an Ebola outbreak in the United States look like? We cannot answer this question — now or in the future, hopefully — from case count data because no such outbreak has occurred.

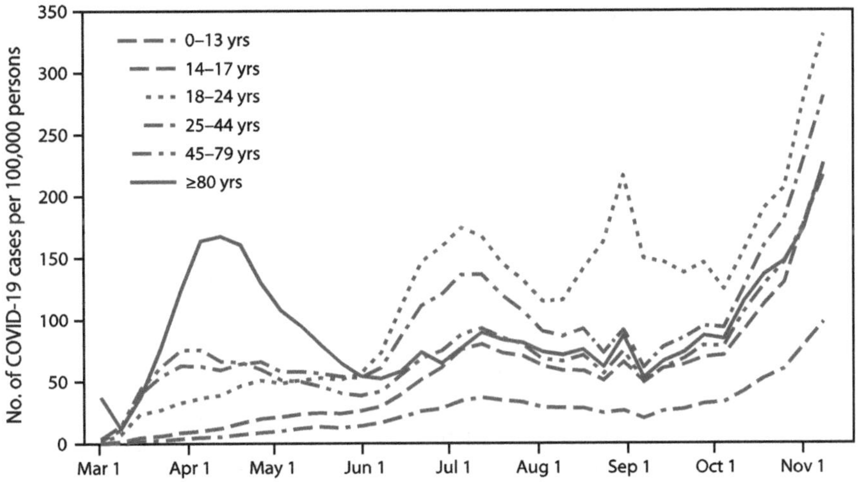

Figure 3.5 Incidence of COVID–19 by age group, USA, 2022

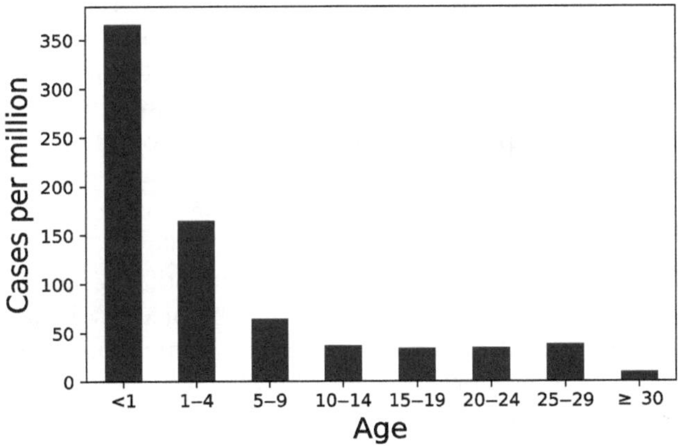

Figure 3.6 Incidence of measles by age group in the European Union during 2017

We could use matrices based on the Western African outbreak, but the very different social structure would make predictions of questionable utility.

In Figure 3.6, we see a relatively large probability of children under the age of one catching measles. This is not, however, related solely to an intrinsic weakness in toddlers or to their position in the social network of proximity (measles is an airborne disease). Rather, it is related to the fact that children of that age are typically too young to have been vaccinated — and 87% of all cases of measles recorded in the European Union in 2017 were unvaccinated.[24] So the development of vaccines against Ebola and COVID–19 are another reason why WAIFW matrices might be of limited future utility — they are contingent on actual vaccine coverage (and efficacy).

Despite these limitations, variations of the WAIFW matrix calibrated on case count have been a workhorse for epidemiologists for many years.

3.5 Why didn't you just ask?

In 2006, Dutch researchers Jacco Wallinga, Peter Teunis, and Mirjam Kretzschmar decided to try a different route to estimate transmission probability between categories of subjects.[25] After all, they reasoned, in order for Lievin to transmit an infectious disease to Nora, they first and foremost needed to make some form of contact. The specific kind of contact might depend from the specific disease (in the case of COVID–19, a few seconds of proximity might suffice); but in general, if Nora talks every day to twice the number of people that Machteld talks to, and the two live in the same region, then it is reasonable to expect that Nora has double the probability that Machteld has of catching any epidemic. This 'reasonable expectation' — which is akin to the $\frac{1}{2}$ assumed for simplicity in the initial simplified examples — was labeled 'social contact hypothesis' by Wallinga and coauthors, who went on to analyze data from a large survey taken years before, in 1986, in the Dutch city of Utrecht. In that survey, 5,000 participants were asked to describe the number and age of people with whom they talked in a typical week. The 2,106 responses obtained allowed the researchers to create 'social contact matrices' with a structure similar to that of WAIFW matrices, and to compare the results to the diffusion of antibodies for the mumps virus.

The approach of asking individuals to describe their social contact was taken to a larger scale by the POLYMOD research project in 2008.[26] This project, financed by the European Commission, consisted of identifying and characterizing the patterns of social contact between citizens of eight European countries, with the explicit goal of modeling the spread of infectious diseases. It was the result of a large international collaboration, but the task was, at its core, simple: ask a large number of subjects (7,290), selected in order to be representative of the population of the countries involved, to describe their encounters on a given day. Each participant was asked to record daily information on individuals they came into contact with during that day; contact could be physical (for example, 'a kiss, or a handshake') or nonphysical (a 'two–way conversation with three or more words'). Importantly, participants were also asked to take note of the gender and the (approximate) age of the other individual. Hence, even though the researchers could not reconstruct the identities of individuals involved in each contact, they could still know the categories they belonged to, which was exactly the information needed to construct matrices analogous to the WAIFW matrices. In total, 97,904 contacts were recorded; wide differences in the number of contacts were observed between countries, with Italians reporting on average 19.77 contacts in a day, compared to the 7.95 for Germans (incidentally providing support to popular stereotypes about the talkativeness of these populations, and partly anticipating the extent of damages caused by COVID–19), but the resulting contact matrices, shown in

Figure 3.7, feature some common, clearly identifiable patterns. These patterns can also be observed in Figure 3.8, a network representation that summarizes all contact matrices produced.

First, there is a clear tendency of people of the same age to make contact, as evidenced by the lighter colors found on the diagonal patterns connecting the bottom left to the upper right corner in Figure 3.7. The second most evident pattern is related to the typical family structure, and consists of two stripes parallel to the main stripe, one above and one below (particularly visible in the matrix for physical contact in Finland). The distance between the stripes mirrors the typical age gap between parents and their offspring — 25–40 years — that is, it signals that family members obviously tend to make contact among themselves. In some countries, one can also spot the hint of a third stripe above the main stripe, close to the 60 years mark, presumably signaling the role of grandparents as care takers for small children.

3.6 Not all societies are created equal

The POLYMOD project was the first to run a large study measuring social contact matrices in a large, reasonably homogeneous region of the world — Europe. But Figure 3.7 makes it clear that despite the common patterns, countries involved in the analysis feature recognizable differences in their contact matrices. Differences can be expected to be even more prominent in countries with very different social characteristics, such as developing countries.

Incidentally, countries with less advanced health systems are precisely those in which diseases can more easily develop into large-scale emergencies, as exemplified by the case of Ebola in Western Africa, so clearly these are the countries for which epidemiological models are of particular urgency. In fact, researchers studying the Ebola outbreak in 2014 employed models based on POLYMOD data, but they were also fully aware that those models were not the best possible tool for the job. In the following years, this has led researchers across the world to replicate the POLYMOD approach in developing countries. A group led by Italian researcher Alessia Melegaro has reconstructed, in collaboration with researchers from Imperial College (United Kingdom) and KEMRI (Kenya), social contact matrices for regions of Zimbabwe and Kenya.[27] One obvious observation suggested by the results (Figure 3.9, referring to Zimbabwe) is that contact is much more frequent with younger individuals: this trivially reflects the much lower life expectancy (31.8 years in Zimbabwe) compared to European countries. We can also observe that while some sketch of the wings is visible, they are much less sharp than in Figure 3.7. This is largely due to the presence of *extended families* in which the age gaps between members are less predictable than in 'standard' European families. In fact, such differences weaken when urban areas of Zimbabwe are considered. In network terms, we can say that the social network between (age groups of) individuals is *less assortative* than those observed in Europe.

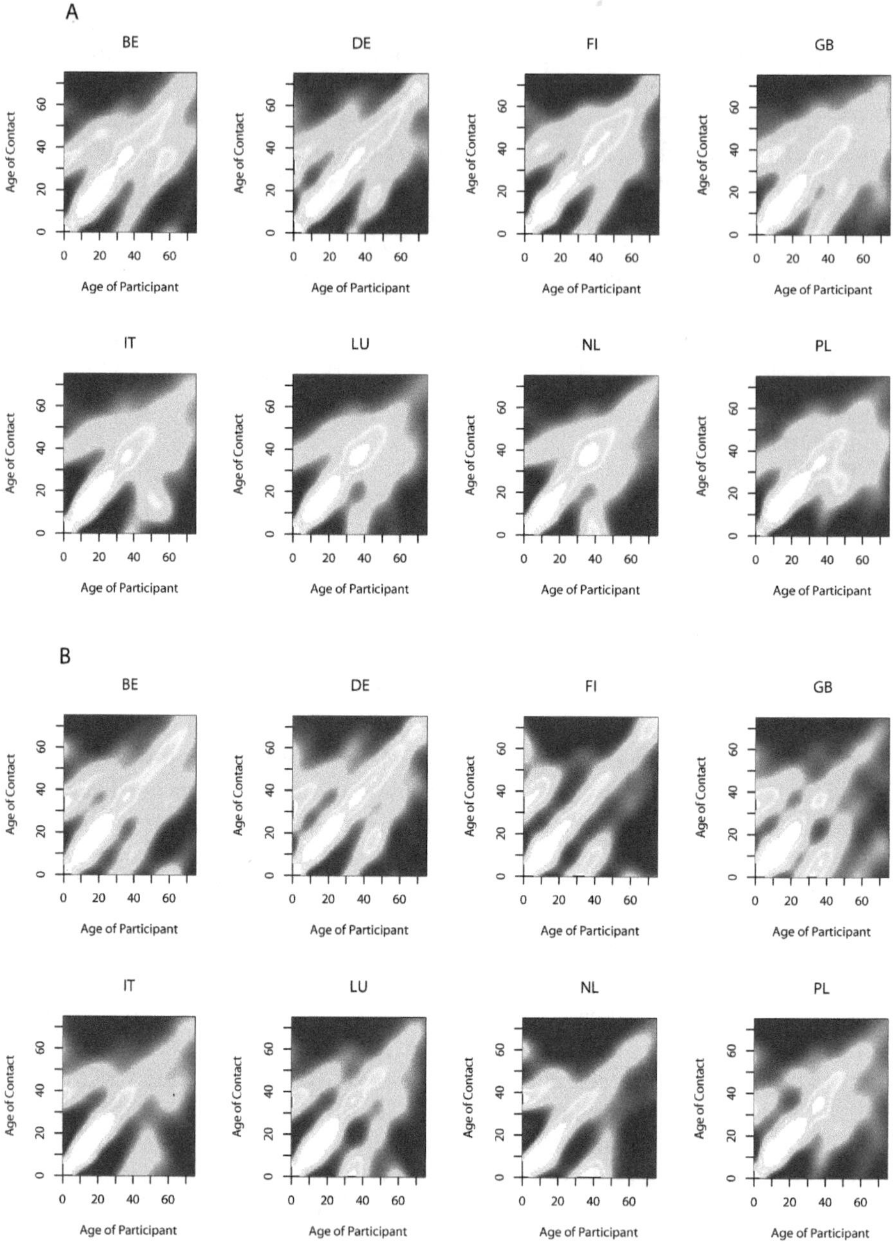

Figure 3.7 Contact matrices from the POLYMOD project. Top (A): all reported contacts; bottom (B): physical contacts

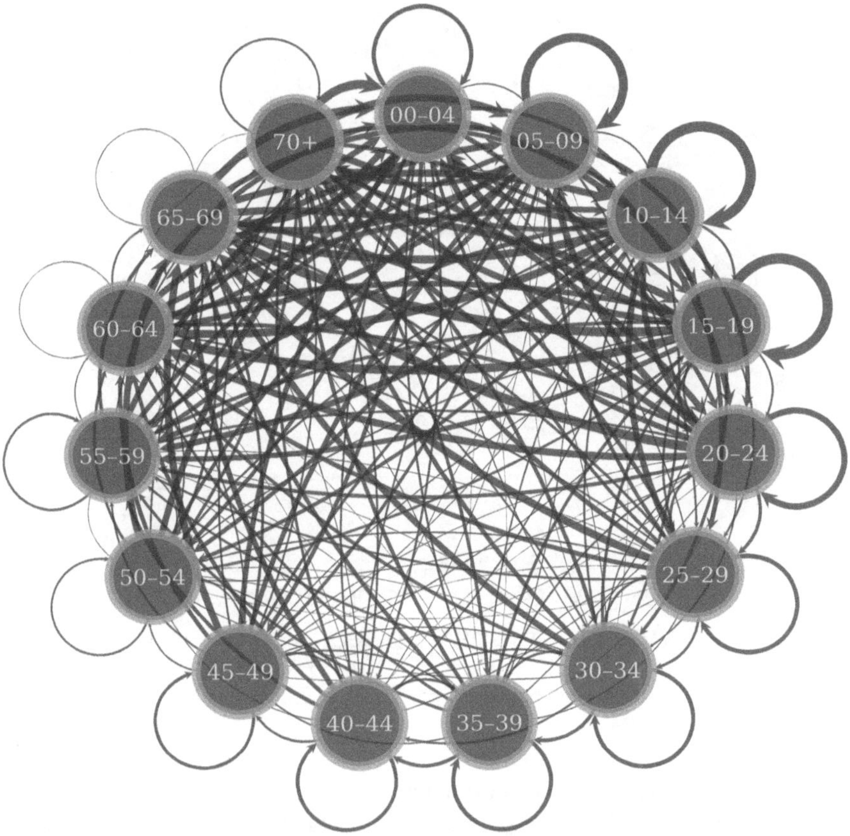

Figure 3.8 Connection intensities between fifteen age classes, from the POLYMOD project (average across countries)

As of today, at least 40 different studies have produced matrices of social contact for different regions of the globe, including Thailand, Vietnam, Cambodia, and Peru, and there is even a website, http://socialcontactdata.org, where several matrices are archived with their data freely available to researchers and officials. This means that when a new outbreak appears, there is a good chance that researchers will be able to simulate its diffusion over a network that closely resembles that of the country affected.

3.7 Age is just a number

Most social contact matrices are based on age, and sometimes gender, despite the fact that other characteristics, such as occupation or sociability, could tell us more about the social life of an individual. Unfortunately, a lot of information that is important for epidemiological contagion is missing in contact

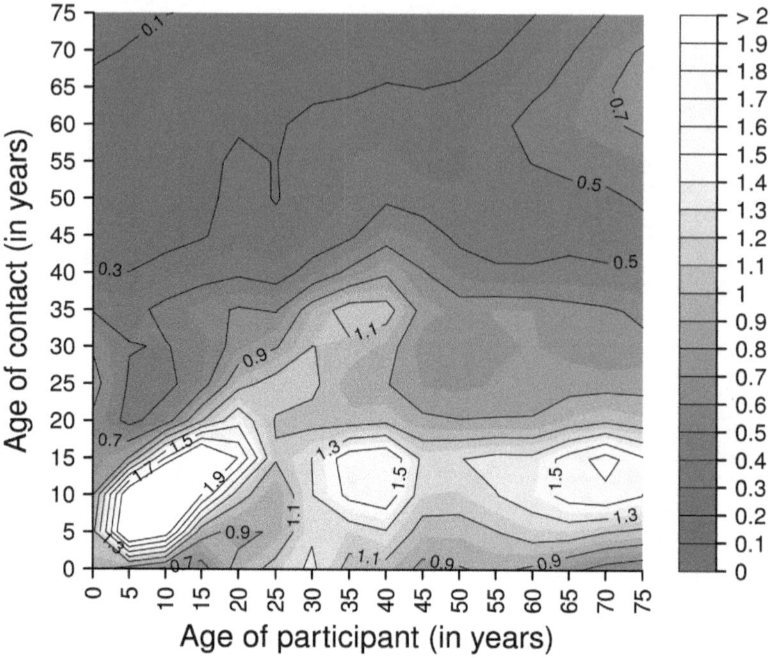

Figure 3.9 Connection intensities between age classes in Zimbabwe

matrices. Not by chance, in most countries, the vaccination campaign against COVID–19 was targeted first and foremost at health workers, and was only afterwards modulated by age groups. Unfortunately, asking people to record the profession and friendliness of people they interact with is much more difficult than asking them to make note of their apparent age and gender. Age can still be a useful measure, however, in that it strongly relates to immunization campaigns (vaccines are typically administered to the population when in infancy) and to susceptibility and vulnerability to diseases (for instance, measles are particularly dangerous for children under 5 years of age[28]). Even so, there is much more to actual social networks than relations between age groups.

It makes sense, then, to examine which aspects of the network of social contact are *not* captured by an age–based social contact matrix. For instance, a 21–year–old university student tends to interact with many other university students of his age every day, but his colleagues are more similar to him (because, for instance, because they too interact with many 21–year–old university students every day) than random 21–years–old individuals. So the real social network of contact has much higher assortativity than that summarized by social contact matrices.

Further, my two 38–year–old best friends do not have the same probability of coming into contact as any two 38–years–old individuals; the odds are much higher that my two friends will interact due to their connection to me. So the real social network of contact has much higher clustering than that summarized by social contact matrices.

Finally, there are no stars in social contact matrices. There are age groups with more reported contacts (such as adolescents), and it is possible to calculate centrality measures for each group, but this does not account for the presence of differences, *within* groups, in the number and type of contacts.

Against these limitations, researchers have tried to complement social contact matrices with a radically different approach. Rather than getting approximate measures of social contact in very large populations (countries), they have focused on obtaining very accurate representations of social contact in smaller groups, by actually recording contacts. The study on romantic relationships among school students, mentioned in Chapter 1, is similar to this approach, but in the case of airborne diseases, recent technologies in the form of lightweight, low power (RFID) proximity sensors have made the task of measuring contact much simpler. In several studies, participants were provided RFID sensors that log an event if two participants are less than 1.5 meters from one another for a given number of seconds — that is, if the two participants holding the sensors engage in a face–to–face interaction. This method is clearly inapplicable to entire countries, but it has been implemented in some public contexts that are interesting for infectious diseases, such as conferences and even a primary school.[29] Pilot studies have applied the same approach to small samples of individuals during their normal daily lives.[30]

The goal of these studies (which incidentally produce stunning graphics, such as those observable on http://sociopatterns.org) is to try to find general network characteristics that are relatively stable across contexts. In contrast to social contact matrices, they can answer questions such as: How differentiated is the degree across a community? How strong is the propensity for friends of my friends to be my friends?

These questions might remind us of the ones we already asked in Chapter 1, for which we *thought* we had an answer: online social networks, a huge, and increasing, archive of social relations, in network form. But the truth is that friendship on Facebook is very different from actual friendship, which itself is no guarantee of frequent social contact. When studying the diffusion of diseases, interaction through posts, comments, and likes is quite different from physical interaction. And remember the average distance in the Facebook friendship network is just 4.57; if the same held for the network of physical contact — or in other words, if every day we met in person all of our Facebook friends, including those who live on the other side of the globe – epidemics would pose an much greater risk for the survival itself of the human species.

This said, one digital technology that made the headlines during the first phase of the COVID–19 pandemic, precisely targeted at reconstructing the network of contagion, is contact tracing *apps*. Dozens of such apps were deployed around the globe, the vast majority of them virtually disappearing from circulation already during 2020, a few months after their introduction. Initially, digital tracking raised high hopes, based on news from a few Eastern countries where its use, albeit raising serious privacy issues, appeared to help governments track and limit the contagion. This was the case for instance in South Korea, where movements of positive individuals (recorded without the need of an app because of device tracking data being available to the government) were *ex–post* made publicly accessible. In Western countries a debate quickly followed on the degree to which privacy could be sacrificed in order to slow down contagion: a heartfelt debate, but relatively superficial. Despite the data under discussion — essentially GPS records, and interactions with other subjects — being routinely collected by Big Tech companies for less noble uses (such as targeted advertising), in most countries it was soon decided (under the auspices of two such companies — Google and Apple) that governments would have obtained as little data as possible. Indeed, while apps based on the 'Exposure Notification' protocol (or similar ones, such as DP–3T) ultimately helped reconstructing a (very small) number of contacts of positive subjects, they provided no help whatsoever — by design — in understanding more in general how the virus was spreading in the population, neither in real time, nor afterwards. Indeed, apps implementing the protocol would not allow the reconstruction of a social network (contacts are known only when positivity of an individual is ascertained, and only to potentially infected individuals), and not even a WAIFW matrix.

In the case of the European Union, several commentators correctly observed that privacy laws (GDPR) impose limits upon the possibility of data collection via such apps. For instance, in Italy, the privacy authority released a statement emphasizing the 'purpose limitation': data on users should have been collected only for the stated purposes — and only to the extent that the collected data was strictly required for these purposes. The problem is that there never was a serious debate on *what* the purposes should be — for instance on whether or not a better understanding of the network on which COVID–19 expands could be considered a legitimate purpose. The fact that apps would not even *allow* individuals to opt–in for a more substantial sharing of data is ironic if we consider that the same European governments that had spent money — via the European Union — on projects like POLYMOD, trying to understand the network of social contact in order to tackle future hypothetical diseases, were now refusing to even consider the possibility of using their apps to better understand a present, and cataclysmic, pandemic — for free.

By the way, contact tracing apps were perfected, but not invented, during the COVID–19 pandemic. In 2011, two scientists, Jon Crowcroft and Eiko Yoneki, had developed *FluPhone*, an app using Bluetooth signals to detect proximity between smartphones, with the declared intent of tracking the spread of flu within Cambridge University. However, 'fewer than one percent of people in Cambridge signed up to use it'.[31] Later, the *BBC Pandemic* project, run between 2017 and 2018, distributed an app which would memorize the position of users, leaving to them the task of manually recording contacts they had with other individuals, over a period of 24 hours. This time, 40,177 participants completed the study, allowing for the construction of contact matrices for the United Kingdom that were later used to study the diffusion of COVID–19.[32]

3.8 Long–haul infections

Today, researchers have the tools to characterize social contact between groups (such as age groups) inside societies, and to observe what actual contact networks between individuals look like in selected communities. They are able to identify common patterns across regions of the world, and to continuously improve the identification of differences *between* regions of the world. The elephant in the room in this discussion, however, is the increasing interconnectedness between these different regions, made prominent by the diffusion of COVID–19. And even though the speed of diffusion of COVID–19 is unprecedented in recent times, other pandemics, such as Ebola in 2014 or the 2009 H1N1 pandemic ('swine flu'), have been markedly identified as global issues, quickly spreading from region to region through the transportation system.

The possibility that diseases are carried across the globe by passengers of long distance travel is not new to epidemiologists nor to public authorities, per se, but the extent to which this represents a risk for global health has changed dramatically in recent decades. The last outbreak of cholera in the United States happened in 1911, when a ship coming from Naples (a city which was known to be affected by a cholera outbreak) arrived in New York with some passengers showing symptoms of the disease. Such passengers were quarantined on Swinburne Island and Hoffman Island, two small artificial islands in the Lower New York Bay. In total, eleven people died — most of them, passengers of the ship — but contagion to the mainland was almost entirely avoided (only two cases were able to avoid quarantine, but they died on the mainland without spreading the infection further). By imposing quarantine on suspect patients, health authorities likely saved thousands of lives. But this was only possible because the ship had taken several days to cross the Atlantic Ocean, and hence cholera symptoms had had the time to make themselves known. Today, a flight from Italy to New York takes less than ten hours, way less than the typical timespan between the ingestion of the bacteria and the appearance of the first symptoms (of course, it is worth mentioning that Italy does not currently host cholera outbreaks); and unfortunately, COVID–19 is contagious even *before* the first symptoms appear. Not only do humans travel faster than they did in the past, but they also travel more. This poses an entire set of new problems for health officials, who must coordinate, and facilitate the sharing of real–time information. In the first stages of the COVID–19 epidemic, some countries seemed to fare worse than others, with Italy for instance being hit particularly hard, and particularly soon. But the general failure was the very limited extent to which different countries were able to coordinate their efforts — in a context in which coordination was crucial. Viruses are no more infectious across national borders than within; but given the difficulty in articulating a coordinated response, closing the national borders to the movements of people (for instance among members of the European Union) was the obvious choice for many of the affected countries.

The task of applying models and simulations of epidemics to the global level, and of integrating them with the real–time availability of relevant data, is the new challenge in this field. Physicists Alessandro Vespignani leads the international research group behind GLEaM (for 'GLobal Epidemic and Mobility'), a model of global epidemic mobility that exploits three different layers of knowledge about epidemics.[33] First, there are the contact matrices at the regional level. These are then connected, like pieces of a global patchwork, using information we have about international socio–demographic dynamics (such as migration flows). The top layer is then represented by the network of human mobility (first and foremost provided by airplane flights), on which data fortunately abounds. GLEaM combines these layers with a flexible way to specify the characteristics of a disease, such as the transmission channel, and the duration of the infectious period. The researchers have gone as far as to offer a software interface (GLEaMviz) that can be downloaded for free, and used to simulate diseases with the 'desired' features. After describing the characteristics of the disease, its diffusion across the human species can be conveniently observed as colored dots and areas appearing on a world map. Models applying the GLEaM model to the spread of COVID–19 have appeared since the first days of the outbreak,[34] providing forecasts of the international diffusion of the virus.

COVID–19 has sadly reminded us that even the richest and most advanced countries are yet to reach the point in which epidemics are no longer a concern. But there is a sort of serendipitous element in the fact that, in the same years in which low cost flights and improved economic conditions have made quick, long–distance journeys a common reality for a large part of the world's population, be it for leisure or for work, researchers are increasingly able to harness network data and methodologies in a real–time effort to limit the risk of pandemics. If the eradication of several diseases (including polio and smallpox) thanks to vaccines was the health revolution of the mid–twentieth century, the data–based prompt and efficient reaction to epidemics, involving simulation of contagion over complex networks, might be remembered as the first health revolution of the new millennium.

Still, ex–post one could get the impression that in the fight against COVID–19, network science has failed miserably. Why is it that despite all studies on contact matrices and mobility, modern societies were unable to stop such a pandemic before it exploded? It is true that network science has somewhat failed: but not in the sense that its tools were found to be inappropriate, or insufficient, for the task. Despite its applications being instrumental in saving countless lives, network science failed to be adopted as an *obvious* and *fundamental* key of interpretation on behalf of the public opinion and policymakers. Rather than being a simple curiosity, the exponential growth described above has a precise consequence: that the utility of any control measure is higher if the control measure is deployed earlier. In the diffusion of a deadly infective disease, detecting and isolating a single infective individual can potentially save a large number of lives. And since it is unthinkable to send an entire nation in lockdown as soon as a single case is observed, interventions must be not just timely, but also focused, employing detailed and up–to–date information.

Unfortunately, many of the actions of decisionmakers did not go in this direction. This is true for Wuhan, and it is true for Western countries as well. Politicians have an incentive to act late, because when things go worse it is easier to make their fellow citizens accept tougher measures (such as lockdowns) — and at the same time to be remembered as a savior. They have an incentive to act with generalized interventions, to not be suspected of favoritism or discrimination (for instance with regional lockdowns, or age–specific vaccination policies). They have an incentive to release as little as possible information and data — including epidemiological data, the analysis of which is paramount — as they fear such evidence could be used against them; and to release them only to a few researchers whom they trust.

Network theory can provide precise indications, but these are of little value if they are not transformed into concrete actions. In order for this to happen, maybe we do not need that concepts such as centrality and average degree are introduced in the syllabus of primary schools, but we definitely need more widespread awareness, among decision makers, that we *are* all parts of a network, and that when some danger flows on this network, we must behave accordingly.

Notes

1 https://cdc.gov/MMWR/preview/mmwrhtml/mm5534a4.htm
2 https://web.archive.org/web/20071003195603/http://aag.org/HDGC/www/health/units/unit4/html/4bkground.html
3 https://cnet.com/how-to/coronavirus-explained-apple-iphone-supply-hurt-cruise-ship-chaos
4 https://technologyreview.com/s/615184/the-coronavirus-is-the-first-true-social-media-infodemic
5 Baize et al., 2014.
6 Apolone et al., 2020; Lai et al., 2020.
7 http://who.int/en/news-room/fact-sheets/detail/ebola-virus-disease
8 Merler et al., 2015.
9 Hui et al., 2020.
10 Auerbach et al., 1984.
11 Worobey et al., 2016.
12 This simplified example ignores the possibility that the neighbors of an infected subject were already infected by another neighbor — and possibly had healed and become immune. This is the cost of basing our analysis solely on such a simple measure as the degree. In any case, for our simple model to work we must assume that the population is large.

13 Strictly speaking, the gambler's ruin argument still rules that sooner or later, and in a large enough population the epidemics will still end spontaneously, but in a game in which the gambler has a significantly larger probability of winning, such eventuality is practically uninteresting.
14 More precisely, the growth rate of the number of infected subjects will *tend* to a constant percentage per day — or will stay constant at it, if such percentage is also the ratio of new cases to old cases at a given moment in time.
15 Pastor-Satorras et al., 2015.
16 Battiston and Gamba, 2021.
17 Guerra et al., 2017.
18 Althaus, 2014.
19 Read et al., 2020.
20 European Centre for Disease Prevention and Control, 2018; European Centre for Disease Prevention and Control, 2019; European Centre for Disease Prevention and Control, 2020.
21 European Centre for Disease Prevention and Control, 2022.
22 Anderson and May, 1992.
23 Even in the presence of detailed data, the calibration of WAIFW matrices requires researchers to make some assumptions — and always leaves them with the doubt of whether these assumptions were correct. The details are complicated, but consider the following example: if cases among toddlers and among adults tend to follow similar trends, how do researchers tell whether it is because adults tend to infect toddlers, or the opposite, or both?
24 Measles and Rubella Surveillance 2017 — European Center for Disease Prevention and Control — https://ecdc.europa.eu
25 Wallinga, Teunis, and Kretzschmar, 2006.
26 Mossong et al., 2008.
27 Melegaro et al., 2017.
28 https://cdc.gov/measles/hcp/index.html
29 Stehlé et al., 2011.
30 Kiti et al., 2016.
31 https://wired.com/story/phones-track-spread-covid19-good-idea
32 Biglarbeigi et al., 2021.
33 Balcan et al., 2010.
34 Chinazzi et al., 2020.

Bibliography

Althaus, Christian L (2014). 'Estimating the reproduction number of Ebola virus (EBOV) during the 2014 outbreak in West Africa'. In: *PLoS Currents* 6.

Anderson, Roy M and Robert M May (1992). 'Infectious diseases of humans: dynamics and control'. Oxford University Press.

Apolone, Giovanni et al. (2020). 'Unexpected detection of SARS-CoV-2 antibodies in the prepandemic period in Italy'. In: *Tumori Journal*, p. 0300891620974755.

Auerbach, David M et al. (1984). 'Cluster of cases of the acquired immune deficiency syndrome: Patients linked by sexual contact'. In: *The American Journal of Medicine* 76.3, pp. 487–492.

Baize, Sylvain et al. (2014). 'Emergence of Zaire Ebola virus disease in Guinea'. In: *New England Journal of Medicine* 371.15, pp. 1418–1425.

Balcan, Duygu et al. (2010). 'Modeling the spatial spread of infectious diseases: The GLobal Epidemic and Mobility computational model'. In: *Journal of Computational Science* 1.3, pp. 132–145.

Battiston, Pietro and Simona Gamba (2021). 'COVID-19: R_0 is lower where outbreak is larger'. In: *Health Policy* 125.2, pp. 141–147.

Biglarbeigi, Pardis et al. (2021). 'Sensitivity analysis of the infection transmissibility in the UK during the COVID-19 pandemic'. In: *PeerJ* 9, e10992.

Chinazzi, Matteo et al. (2020). 'The effect of travel restrictions on the spread of the 2019 novel coronavirus (COVID-19) outbreak'. In: *Science*, 368.6489: 395–400.

European Centre for Disease Prevention and Control (2018). 'Measles and rubella surveillance - 2017'. Tech. rep. https://ecdc.europa.eu/sites/portal/files/documents/Measles-and-Rubella-Surveillance-2017-final_0.pdf. Stockholm.

— (2019). 'Monthly measles and rubella monitoring report – February 2019'. Tech. rep. https://ecdc.europa.eu/sites/default/files/documents/measles-rubella-monthly-monitoring-report-february-2019.pdf. Stockholm.

— (2020). 'Monthly measles and rubella monitoring report – February 2020'. Tech. rep. https://ecdc.europa.eu/sites/default/files/documents/measles-rubella-monthly-report-february-2020.pdf. Stockholm.

— (2022). 'Measles Annual Epidemiological Report for 2022'. Tech. rep. https://ecdc.europa.eu/sites/default/files/documents/MeaslesAnnualEpidemiologicalReport2022data.pdf. Stockholm.

Guerra, Fiona M et al. (2017). 'The basic reproduction number (R_0) of measles: a systematic review'. In: *The Lancet Infectious Diseases* 17.12, pp. e420–e428.

Hui, David S et al. (2020). 'The continuing 2019-nCoV epidemic threat of novel coronaviruses to global health — The latest 2019 novel coronavirus outbreak in Wuhan, China'. In: *International Journal of Infectious Diseases* 91, pp. 264–266.

Kiti, Moses C et al. (2016). 'Quantifying social contacts in a household setting of rural Kenya using wearable proximity sensors'. In: *EPJ Data Science* 5, pp. 1–21.

Lai, Alessia et al. (2020). 'Early phylogenetic estimate of the effective reproduction number of SARS-CoV-2'. In: *Journal of Medical Virology* 92.6, pp. 675–679.

Melegaro, Alessia et al. (2017). 'Social contact structures and time use patterns in the Manicaland Province of Zimbabwe'. In: *PloS One* 12.1, e0170459.

Merler, Stefano et al. (2015). 'Spatiotemporal spread of the 2014 outbreak of Ebola virus disease in Liberia and the effectiveness of non-pharmaceutical interventions: a computational modelling analysis'. In: *The Lancet Infectious Diseases* 15.2, pp. 204–211. ISSN: 1473-3099.

Mossong, Joël et al. (2008). 'Social contacts and mixing patterns relevant to the spread of infectious diseases'. In: *PLoS Medicine* 5.3, e74.

Pastor-Satorras, Romualdo et al. (2015). 'Epidemic processes in complex networks'. In: *Reviews of Modern Physics* 87.3, p. 925.

Read, Jonathan M et al. (2020). 'Novel coronavirus 2019-nCoV: early estimation of epidemiological parameters and epidemic predictions'. In: *medRxiv*.

Stehlé, Juliette et al. (2011). 'High-resolution measurements of face-to-face contact patterns in a primary school'. In: *PloS One* 6.8, e23176.

Wallinga, Jacco, Peter Teunis, and Mirjam Kretzschmar (2006). 'Using data on social contacts to estimate age-specific transmission parameters for respiratory-spread infectious agents'. In: *American Journal of Epidemiology* 164.10, pp. 936–944.
Worobey, Michael et al. (2016). '1970s and 'Patient 0' HIV-1 genomes illuminate early HIV/AIDS history in North America'. In: *Nature* 539.7627, p. 98.

4 Information diffusion as contagion

It should come as no surprise that parallels can be drawn between the diffusion of infectious diseases over social networks of contact and proximity and the diffusion of information over more general social networks, primarily online. Indeed, when a picture, video, ad, or meme rapidly spreads in online communities through person-to-person diffusion, it is said to have gone *viral* — that is, it has propagated like a virus. Today, the word 'virus' itself is used just as often to refer to *computer* viruses — malicious software that spread across our electronic devices — as it is to the original biological meaning.

Figure 4.1a shows the number of views for *Gangnam Style*, the first video ever to break the barrier of one billion views on YouTube.[1] Since then, other videos have surpassed this threshold, and even surpassed *Gangnam Style*, which as of April 2024 ranks tenth among the most viewed videos (fifth, if we disregard children's songs). But the K–pop hit remains an example of how quickly a relatively unknown artist can rise to fame thanks to online word of mouth and the spread of information across digital social networks. Figure 4.1b zooms in on the area of the dashed rectangle of Figure 4.1a using the logarithmic scale we met in the previous chapter (Figure 3.3), which emphasizes the *percentage* change over time. Once again, points are almost aligned — that is, the percentage change is roughly constant — that is, growth is exponential.

This result is to be expected, given that the mechanism of online viral diffusion is quite similar to the diffusion of an actual infectious disease: once a subject is 'infected' by the trending content, he might, with some probability, post/retweet/share the content, 'infecting' some share of his contacts, who then 'infect' some share of their contacts by posting/retweeting/sharing the content, and so on. The growth rate of approximately 6% per day also happens to be comparable to that of diseases discussed in the previous chapter. If there is a difference, it is what happens *after* the phase of exponential growth: in the case of epidemics, it is natural that health authorities and individuals will react — in the case of COVID–19, this includes face masks, social distancing, lockdown and also vaccines — in a way that eventually will lead the curve to flatten (possibly after important fluctuations, such as the 'waves' that characterized the pandemic). In the case of *Gangnam Style*, after the period of exponential

DOI: 10.4324/9781003490951-4

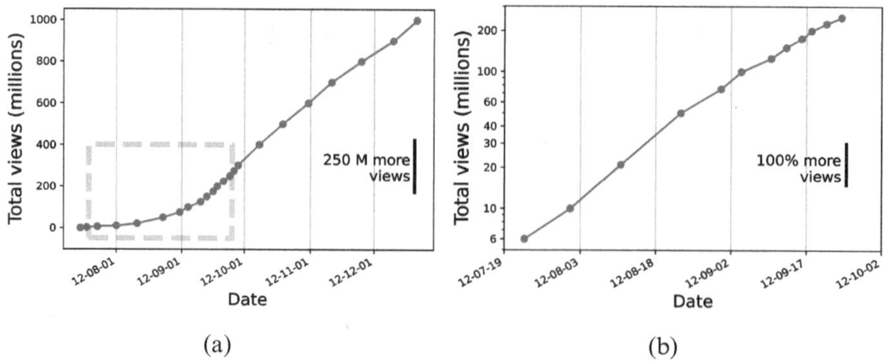

Figure 4.1 Number of views for the *Gangnam Style* video on YouTube

growth, the number of views continued to increase (significantly, given that it passed the mark of three billion views), albeit at a slower pace. Not only was there no effort to 'eradicate' the spread of Gangnam Style, but some users chose to watch the video again, even though they had already seen it at least once before, further increasing the number of views.

As previously discussed, a virus's basic reproduction number is what determines an infective disease's ability to spread; the same approach can be used to try to understand what makes a viral video … viral. We already know that the typical degree in online social networks (for instance the average number of Facebook friends) is much higher than the typical degree in real–life social contact networks (for instance, the number of people a subject typically interacts with physically in a specific period of time). A single click of the 'share' button on Facebook can potentially catapult a picture to more people's dashboards in a single instant than a person tends to meet face–to–face in an entire month. Another important aspect lies in the probability of contagion over each existing edge. Ebola can only spread through body fluids, so even a handshake is typically not enough for contagion to occur; COVID–19 is airborn and spreads more easily. A popular video on Facebook is definitely more similar to COVID–19 than to Ebola: the act of viewing it and possibly sharing it is extremely simple, so if the preview, or the comment accompanying the video, is intriguing enough, a sizable portion of them presumably will. Moreover, incubation time, a crucial factor in determining the speed of diffusion of an epidemic, is potentially null: if a person receives a YouTube link from a friend, that person might share it in a matter of minutes, or even seconds. This does not, in principle, affect the overall number of cases or views; but it does explain the speed at which internet phenomena rise (and fall, once their novelty is a thing of the past).

Videos from individuals who already have an established reputation, such as famous pop singers, often reach a large number of views, too, but they follow very different growth patterns, because many fans likely subscribe to the famous individual's feed and receive an immediate notification, while the initial exposure of others to the song might come from the radio or television — in neither case exploiting the 'contagiousness' of online networks. In fact, YouTube uses an algorithm to identify viral videos at the beginning of their diffusion — that is, when they reach 10,000 views[2] — allowing the platform to offer video creators a deal for sharing subsequent advertising revenues. This algorithm is possible because the spread of viral content follows specific growth patterns, which can in part be predicted.

4.1 A penny for your tweets

Music tastes may vary, but while the *Gnangnam Style* 'infection' is clearly nowhere near as dangerous as an infection from Ebola, plague or COVID–19, there are very good reasons for researchers and governments to understand, and monitor the propagation of content over online social networks. This chapter is dedicated to explaining, from the vantage point of network theory, why it is important that researchers and governments are able to understand and monitor the propagation of information in online social networks. By the way, there are a myriad of private individuals and companies for which analyzing online social networks is an important business — a business whose interest may often conflict with that of users.

Similar to infectious diseases, after grasping the general features of the social network over which information spreads, the natural next step is to understand how differences *across* the network shape this kind of contagion. We know already that the average X or Facebook account has a large number of edges compared to networks of physical interaction, but one even more striking difference between 'virtual' and 'physical' networks lies in the heterogeneity across individuals. The POLYMOD project mentioned in Chapter 3 found that the average number of daily, in person contacts was 13.4 among all countries involved. While this is clearly only an average, and one must account for the presence of nodes with smaller or larger degrees — such as toddlers on one side and health workers on the other — also depending on the type of connection studied (physical contact, or verbal interaction), it is still reasonable to expect that people talk to at least two other individuals and no more than a couple of hundred people, every day.

But consider for a moment the extreme case of an *exceptionally* busy shop seller who gets one customer every ten seconds for eight hours of work. At the end of the working day, he will have interacted with more than two thousand customers. The difference between two and two thousand seems substantial, but it is minimal when compared to the heterogeneity across X accounts: many of which have no followers at all, while some have tens of millions of followers. These accounts with enormous numbers of followers are expected to give their owners a tremendous amount of influence — indeed, that of the 'influencer' is one of the key roles in new approaches to marketing. But how can this influence actually be measured? Try (or better: imagine) standing in a square and shouting to all passers-by your political opinions: at the end of the day, you might have 'established contact' — in some sense, at least — with many of them, but it is not clear to what extent you have 'influenced' anyone. Instead, following a X account is the result of a choice, which implies some level of interest, or trust.

Reading people's X feeds is much easier than reading the minds of passers-by's minds. From this, an important stream of research has developed to analyze *cascades* of information over online social networks, that is, how one user's tweets or posts have an influence on her followers' or friends' tweets or posts.

One thing to keep in mind is that while biological viruses remain mostly identifiable (the Ebola and SARS–CoV–2 viruses, for instance, are ultimately recognized, even across mutations, by their RNA), information that flows over online social networks takes much less predictable forms. The example of the *Gangnam Style* video is relatively simple: either a web user visits its URL or not. Either a tweet links to it or not. But what about the incessant, feverish exchange of opinions, comments, and replies to comments constantly taking place on online social platforms? Today, online debate undeniably plays an important role in shaping opinions, but 'opinions' are not as easily tracked as a viral video.

Luckily for researchers who study contagion in online social networks, the inclusion of URLs inside tweets, posts and messages is a relatively common way to refer to someone else's opinion, or even to express one's own thoughts. In 2011, researchers from Yahoo! Research analyzed more than one billion tweets, identifying 1.6 million independent 'cascades' over the network of followers[3] — that is, events in which one user posted an image by including its URL, and then some followers reposted it, and so on.[4] Each cascade had a 'seed' — what would be 'index case' in an epidemic outbreak — and then could be tracked along the edges of the 'who follows who' network.

Figure 4.2 shows one of the 1.6 million cascades detected by the study, and an arrow indicates the actual act of reposting the same image, not the mere fact of being a follower. It is a particular type of network, one that is directed, and typically has *no loops* — users do not often retweet the same content *twice* (contrast this, for instance with Figure 3.4). Networks satisfying this property are called 'Directed Acyclic Graphs' (or DAGs) and have important applications in several different disciplines — for instance, in a hydraulic network that distributes water to homes, water does not go around in circles.

The X cascades discussed here are an instance in which, as discussed in Chapter 1, the description of a network is not composed solely by nodes (users/tweets) and arrows (being a follower), but also of *time*. If Hassan is a follower of Kim, Kim is often a follower of Hassan. But if first Hassan tweets an image of a funny cat and then Kim does the same a few minutes later, it is very likely that it was Hassan who influenced Kim, rather than the other way around. Hence, the fact that tweets are precisely timestamped is an important part of the analysis that allows the construction of figures such as Figure 4.2.

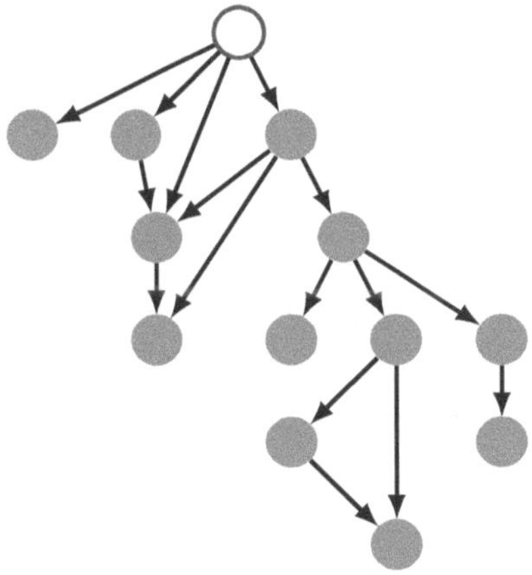

Figure 4.2 An example of a cascade over X

Timing was also important in reconstructing the spread of COVID–19, but in that case a time resolution of one day was sufficient, as it was well below the typical incubation time — while as already mentioned, the incubation time for the sharing of online contents is virtually null.

The vast majority of cascades are smaller than the one represented in Figure 4.2 — in fact, they barely deserve the designation of 'cascade'. Other studies by Yahoo! researchers have shown that this is not a specificity of X.[5] Some cascades are much bigger instead involving thousands, or even tens of thousands of nodes. But the number of small cascades is so large that they end up being responsible for the vast majority of 'observed' influence. As the Yahoo! researchers note, this is markedly different from what is typically observed for infectious diseases, where for instance '*the majority of all humans who have ever been infected with avian influenza were infected during a single event, namely the 1918 pandemic, during which more than 500 million individuals are thought to have been infected*'. This is even more true if we compare *different* diseases: rather than many small epidemics, we tend to have few very large ones (think about COVID–19 or AIDS). This has to do with the fact that human beings tend to differ in their *tastes* more than in the characteristics of their bodies: so while an infective disease is likely to be dangerous for everybody, what a X user shares needs not be of interest of many others.

The importance of the many small cascades suggests that when we examine a single, huge viral phenomenon such as the diffusion of a top hit video, we are really only seeing the tip of the iceberg of diffusion and influence over online social networks. Influence is more diffused than influenza.

The studies mentioned only analyze one social network at a time, disregarding the fact that many people with an X account might also have accounts on TikTok *and* WhatsApp *and* other online platforms and messaging apps. If my friend Romeo, whom I follow, tweets a video that I find compelling, I might

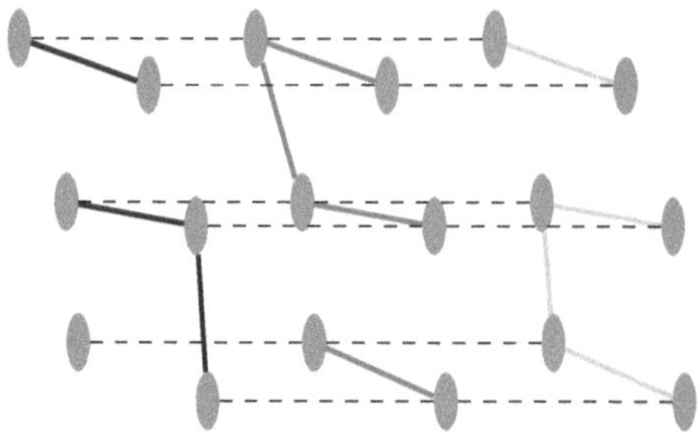

Figure 4.3 An example of a multiplex network made of six nodes connected over three different layers

immediately share the URL with the Facebook group of my work colleagues; then a colleague of mine might share it on TikTok, and her friend Juliet might in turn include it in a tweet. But unless Juliet is also a follower of Romeo on X, this contagion will go unobserved to a researcher examining any of these social networks in isolation. Networks in which nodes can be linked by different *types*, or *layers*, of links (for instance Romeo and I can follow each other on X *and* be Facebook friends *and* chat via Telegram, see Figure 4.3) are called 'multiplex networks', and a growing body of tools and methodologies are being developed for their analysis. But in the case of online social networks, the real obstacle to their analysis is simply reconstructing them. Identifying Romeo's followers on X is an easy task. Identifying Romeo's Facebook friends can also be an easy task (depending on Romeo's privacy settings). The same applies to identifying Romeo's Instagram circles. But the really difficult thing is tracing Romeo's X, Facebook, and Instagram accounts back to the same individual. This is an obstacle not just for independent researchers, but also for research teams working within the social platforms themselves.

Another important thing to consider is that URLs, hashtags, retweets and shares are clearly identifiable signs that simplify the study of influence, but they are certainly not the only way to communicate on social networks. In recent years, there has been a large increase of studies on the *sentiment analysis* of user produced content: or, in other words, employing *Natural Language Processing* (NLP) techniques to extract meaning from free text. The task is made more difficult by the frequent use of abbreviations, context–specific jargon and acronyms in online discussions, which also provide little context for the discussion (consider the 280 character limit for tweets).

Therefore, interpreting text is a significantly more difficult task than tracking references to a URL, the extreme example being that of *irony* (which, not by chance, is a powerful tool to work around automatic censorship in place like China, for instance[6]). A tweet containing the sentence 'How lucky we are to live in a city which such a nice weather!' will be interpreted in a radically different way depending on what city the user lives in — a fact that is probably obvious to most of her followers, but not necessarily to an algorithm trying to interpret the tweet. In any case, the application of NLP to social networks is an exciting direction of research, because it potentially allows for studies of opinion diffusion over online social networks of radically larger breadth than those mentioned so far. For instance, only by interpreting text can we really understand how users of social networks influence each other's political views — forming cascades that are large, complex, and much harder to identify than memes.

In general, online social networks can be studied at different levels of analysis. There is the level of the network itself, defined as one profile being a friend, or follower, of another. The second level is defined by actual interactions at the local level, such as retweeting, replying, and liking. The third level concerns how a specific content spreads in a social network, for instance, by mapping which part of the Facebook social network is 'infected' by *Gangnam Style*, or some hashtag. The three levels can be seen as roughly analogous, respectively, to the social contact matrix, the WAIFW matrix, and the actual study of the diffusion of COVID–19. And all are important to understanding the potentialities and risks of online social networks as the new mass media — or at least, as crucial complements to mass media.

Before proceeding to some of the more thorny aspects of online contagion, it is worth remembering that the act of 'influencing' other individuals is almost never without side effects — and the effects, as seen in Chapter 2 can go beyond these 'other individuals'. Consider again Figure 4.2: we do not know which image the cascade was referring to, but it certainly must have caught some interest, because after the seed user posted it, thirteen other users did the same (potentially reaching thousands of total viewers). It might have been an animated gif of a kitten playing with a ball of yarn – in which case it might have brought a bit of relief and some smiles to people during a boring subway commute, or work meeting. It might have been the picture of a bike, stolen from some friend of the seed user, and finally found on the street by another user reached by the cascade. Or it might have been a picture of a blue sky with white airplane trails and a tagline assuming the CIA is using these trails to spread chemicals. In any of these cases, the cascade most certainly reached users unknown to the seed user, triggering reactions or feelings that she did not anticipate. The ease with which content can be reached and shared over online platforms makes these virtual social networks an externalities paradise.

4.2 Partisan cascades

Memes are much often studied more because they are easy to identify than because of their intrinsic importance. Other cascades — cascades in which the content is meant to inform rather than just amuse — have a much more immediate impact on the political discourse. Cascades of information are something that social scientists desperately need to understand — not only to satisfy intellectual curiosity, but also because they are shaping the way today's democratic systems function.

Multiple parallels can be drawn — and have already been drawn, in this chapter — between the diffusion of epidemics and the diffusion of information over social networks. But one difference is clear: information is often used maliciously — or at least, strategically, depending on one's point of view. This difference was evident long before Internet existed: referring to Nazi false flag operations meant to present the 1939 invasion of Poland by Germany as a reaction to Polish provocations, Adolf Hitler said, 'The victor will not be asked afterward whether he told the truth or not'. [7]

Yes, infectious diseases have also been used as weapons, both in medieval times by Mongol forces besieging the city of Caffa[8] and in World War II by Japanese forces in China,[9] not to mention the development of chemical weapons. In 2014, health workers in Ebola–affected Guinea succumbed not just to the virus, but on at least one occasion to the violent reaction of villagers who accused them of spreading the disease,[10] and things have gotten even worse for health workers fighting the 2018 Congo outbreak.[11] COVID–19 brought to the forefront the sometimes violent opposition between those who fight, in the name of various conspiracy theories, against control measures, and health authorities, all the while experts all around the world struggle to convince parents that compulsory vaccines are not a conspiracy of 'big pharma' lobbies. Despite all of this, historically humanity has stood mostly united, although with varying levels of effort and competence, when it comes to combating diseases, to the extent that the use of biological warfare is today recognized as a war crime. The same cannot be said, however, for the diffusion of false information.

At the risk of sounding naive, it is useful to frame the specificities of information contagion by asking *why* information today is in one way or another so easily manipulated.

One obvious reason might be that creating false information is easy – easier than growing plague–infected fleas, for instance. It requires a bit of fantasy and know–how, but no specific laboratories or technologies. Another reason is that the boundary between 'true' and 'false' information is blurred, which does not mean there is no right or wrong, but rather, like with the shades of gray between black and white, there is no obvious or universally recognized threshold between right and wrong. There are standardized tests that can tell with almost certainty if an individual is infected by plague, HIV, measles, or COVID–19; but judging to what extent a piece of information provides a genuine representation of the world is occasionally difficult, always hard to automatize, and in some cases outright impossible.

There is a third reason, however, for why information today is so easily manipulated — one that is more related to the environment in which information flows than to the nature itself of information, and one that bears a fundamental role in explaining the recent resurgence of the problem of fake news: historically, information has often been linked to *power*. From secret services and state control of the press, to market–driven phenomena such as the concentration of media ownership in the hands of large holdings and the importance of trade secrets, the ability to spread or hide information often represents a consequence of, or a prerequisite to, power. The result of this, and of the multitude of forms that censorship and colluded press have taken in the history of humanity, is a certain distrust of 'official' sources and authorities (often including the scientific community) and an urge to believe, and propagate, 'alternative' information — first and foremost for its independence from and opposition to *'what they want you to believe'*, and only secondly because of its content. In other words, fake news and 'alternative facts' are a serious problem for modern democracies because their chaotic, uncontrolled and authority–free mode of propagation is instinctively seen as an asset, not as a problem, by participants.

After all, one can almost understand why some parents embrace the fake news concerning vaccines when their children begin to show signs of autism around the age of three: unable to heal their offspring, they desperately cling to an explanation that — despite being false, originating from a fraudulent research article and discredited by experts — would at least provide some explanation beyond pure chance.

But how can we explain the persistence with which multitudes of individuals – inside and outside the United States — have kept the Moon landing conspiracy alive, claiming that manned landings between 1969 and 1972 were staged? Very few people (really, only professional conspiracy theorists) have a personal interest in disproving the fact that twelve people in bulky white NASA suits were able, many years ago, to walk on the moon. In the midst of the Cold War, spreading skepticism about the American space program could have been considered a cunning strategy on behalf of the Soviet Union, but even then no such attempt was made by communist forces, possibly because the evidence was considered irrefutable.

The diffusion of these and other conspiracy theories can exploit basic human psychological traits, such as the desire to explain incomprehensible phenomena (as in the case of the vaccine–autism link) or to connect apparently counterintuitive theories to personal observation, or religious beliefs (as in the case of 'flat earth' societies). But all conspiracy theories are linked, and strongly driven, first and foremost by the desire to contrast the 'official truth' with writings that incite the reader to 'think critically'.

Claiming that fake news 'just happens' spontaneously because of the gullibility of people would be deceitful: fake news is instrumental in promoting specific interests, and sometimes its dissemination is carefully planned and fostered. But the ease with which fake news and its creators gain a foothold in the realm of public opinion, and the influence they have on the functioning of modern societies, is related to the fact that word of mouth and critical thinking *are* powerful antidotes to propaganda and censorship of any kind.

While this might seem like a purely philosophical issue, it is directly related to the difficulty of fighting the spread of false information online: even if done in good faith, censorship is problematic and inevitably bears the risk not just of suppressing valid information sources, but also of fortifying skepticism in regards to those valid sources. In an unexpected twist of metaphoric and medical contagion phenomena, Chinese censorship has faced significant difficulties in controlling the spread of information about the COVID–19 outbreak that began in Wuhan in December 2019.[12]

4.3 The dark side of 'free' information

The recent emergence of the expression 'fake news' in the public discourse does not mean we have only recently discovered that false information can be used maliciously; examples of this have always abounded. It is instead directly related to the profound, and abrupt, change in the way citizens of advanced economies access information. And it ultimately has more to do with how information is *diffused* than with how it is *created.*

Precisely because identifying the degree of truth of a piece of information is a difficult task, the *reputation* of information sources has always been a crucial aspect of acquiring credible news about the world. And until very recently, setting up a news outlet — be it a newspaper, a radio station, or a television channel — was a costly enterprise. This created a virtuous circle (not without exceptions, obviously) in which highly reputed media had a strong incentive to protect their credibility, and by extension their business interests, by publishing dependable and honest news; at the same time, users tended to coalesce around the few relevant media they considered trustworthy. If one had to draw the flow of information, it would look similar to the star network drawn in Figure 1.10b. But in recent years, as summarized by an article, 'The science of fake news', written by political scientist David Lazer with an impressive cast of coauthors (the article poses the question of how to use science to counteract fake news, and admits that the answer is yet to be found), *'the internet has lowered the cost of entry to new competitors [...] and undermined the business models of traditional news sources that had enjoyed high levels of public trust and credibility'.*[13]

That the internet has lowered the cost of entry for new media sources might seem trivial: websites are certainly cheaper than rotary presses. But the main reason why competing with the big players is easier today for new entrants is not only related to the cost of setting up a news outlet and filling it with content; it is also related to the difficulty of *reaching* a new audience, which is now immensely lower thanks to the internet. Traditionally, newspapers' customer bases have been rather loyal, in part because the number of big competitors was limited, but also in part because of a more physical limitation: there was no way to make a (photo)copy of an article and physically send it to hundreds of friends scattered around the globe, all in a matter of seconds.

This is exactly what has happened with online newspapers and online social networks. The ease of access to news websites might have undermined the competitive advantage of established newspapers; but it is the 'like', 'share', 'retweet', and 'forward' buttons that have allowed new entrants to make a splash. They have completely changed the way of consuming information, from a direct relationship between an information source and a consumer, to a process of diffusion over social networks. If the content of a web page is appealing enough for users of online social networks, or of messaging apps, to spread it among their contacts, then publicity is free — and it increases exponentially.

One could argue that discussing the news with friends, family members, and colleagues is not a new phenomenon, but rather an established habit in many communities — and arguably a pillar of any healthy democracy. However, there are several important differences between discussing the news with friends sitting in a pub and sharing content via online social networks. The first has already been mentioned: the typical number of daily physical contacts (based on the POLYMOD data) is between seven and twenty, while the typical number of Facebook friends, or X followers, can easily be orders of magnitude higher. Second, when discussing the news in a bar, it is easier to actually state one's opinion than to cite verbatim a newspaper article, while precisely the opposite is true on Facebook, where sharing or liking takes one or two clicks in total, while articulating an opinion is less immediate — particularly from mobile devices. The third difference is that news sources are much better able to gather feedback about the impact of their news, and to strategically use the resulting insights when producing new content.

The fact that opinion diffusion over social networks can be quicker, more anonymous, and at the same time easier to track, is not necessarily bad. The problem is if users still *act* like they are debating with their friends at the pub about the information read in the newspaper, while in fact they typically do not know the origin of the news they read, they do not appreciate the extent of cascades they take part in, and oftentimes, they do not even know with whom they are debating. This can bite in two different ways. On one hand, a user might trust people he does not actually know. On the other hand, he might assume that people he knows are representative of opinions present in the population, but this is almost never true because the social network around the user exhibits clustering, and assortativity.

4.4 More — or less — than simple nodes

It is difficult to say whether or not Jenna Abrams will be remembered in any history book. True, this young American girl's often inflammatory tweets garnered her a lot of attention (and more than seventy thousand followers, easily placing her among the 1% of most followed Twitter accounts) during the 2016 US presidential campaign. With a bio stating 'I'm not pro–Trump. I'm pro–common sense', she tweeted statements like 'Did you know that the flag and the *[Civil]* war wasn't about slavery, it was all about money', which earned her rebuttals from historians (like Kevin Kruse, a Princeton professor), from a former US ambassador to Russia (Michael McFaul), and from the host of an award–winning radio show dedicated to investigative journalism (Al Letson); even a soon–to–be national security adviser (Michael Flynn) retweeted a post of hers. And obviously, such publicity attracted yet more followers. Her tweets were cited by a large number of important media outlets, including the *New York Times*, the *Washington Post*, the BBC, the *Independent*, and many others.[14]

However her Twitter account was later deleted, and the mentions of her tweets removed from most of the articles that had cited her.[15] All for a simple reason: she did not actually exist.

Jenna Adams was a creation of the Internet Research Agency, a company based in Saint Petersburg, Russia, which made the news in 2017 as the 'troll factory'. Already in 2015, it employed at least a thousand people in a single building — and many more remotely — with the precise aim of influencing public opinion, both domestic and in other countries, on a large range of policy issues. Its employees did so by creating and managing thousands of fake accounts on online social networks, in a strategy that Twitter (now X) connected to the Kremlin.[16] According to a whistle–blower's report, these fake accounts participated vigorously not only in the 2016 US presidential elections, strongly supporting the candidacy of Donald Trump, but also in several other debates, including an energetic campaign to leave the European Union in the lead up to the 2016 UK referendum on Brexit.[17]

Investigations on Russian interferences in US political elections — already taking place years before the 2022 Russian invasion of Ukraine would definitely deteriorate the relationships between the two countries — have filled countless pages of newspapers. But political elections in other countries are by no mean immune: in proximity to the 2024 elections of the European Parliament, 193 pro–Kremlin sites were (re)activated just in French, with the aim of steering the vote towards anti–European and pro–Russian parties. And the problem of authenticity of X accounts is way more general.

The existence of fake Twitter accounts was not a revelation of the troll factory's whistle–blower per se. Already in the 2010 US midterm elections, researchers had observed in action coordinated pools of accounts run by *bots* — that is, automated programs, posting, following and retweeting as if they were actual people. The same researchers even developed automated detection tools to identify such bots. These tools work by analyzing a wide range of characteristics for each node/account; interestingly, the features that better differentiate fake bot accounts from genuine accounts are related more to the position of the account in the network of followers than to the actual content of the tweets.[18]

Similar detection tools helped assess the relevance of the huge *ghost followers* industry, through which Twitter personalities increase their followers count simply by paying a fee to private companies. One of these private companies was, at a given moment, managing approximately 3.5 million automated accounts, producing a total of more than two hundred million followers for its customers.[19] The detection tools made it possible to systematically identify Twitter personalities who enrolled armies of ghost followers, and the list included actors, athletes, politicians, activists, and even the crown prince of Saudi Arabia (this last, not for mere vanity, but with the aim of supporting domestic stances in the killing of journalist Jamal Khashoggi in 2018).[20] The troll factory scandal, given its political implications, directed unprecedented attention to the problem of fake accounts, and Twitter itself, again using automated detection tools, reportedly deleted fifty–eight million fake accounts in the last three months of 2017 alone.[21] These clean–up campaigns periodically result in drops in the number of followers for even 'regular' accounts, which suggests that one of the ways bots maintain a semblance of normalcy is by following accounts that are not on their master's payroll.[22] In other words, given that detection tools analyze the network position of accounts, accounts attempt to make their network positions appear 'normal'.

The identification and deletion of dozens of millions of fake X accounts should in principle be good news because it helps clean up the environment where millions of *real* people form their opinions. But in this game of cops and robbers, the robbers will always have an advantage: that creating a fake X account is much easier than identifying one. The number of deleted accounts might reassure advertisers and investors, but it is not a guarantee that no or few fake accounts remain; on the contrary, there are reports of bot accounts living undisturbed for several years, surviving multiple clean–up campaigns.[23] And while Elon Musk, before completing the acquisition of Twitter (later renamed to X) in October 2022, had put a particular emphasis on the problem of fake accounts, the decision to cease its identity verification program in April 2024, replacing it with a paid program, dealt an immediate and lasting blow to credibility and identifiability on the platform, immediately leading to a number of fake profiles using the $ 8 'blue check' to inspire trustworthiness.

Most importantly, while the techniques to identify bots on X and Facebook have improved dramatically — and will probably improve further, as bots themselves increase in sophistication — this does not solve the 'Jenna Abrams problem'. What is known about the Russian company behind that fake X account (and many more) only came to light because Russian activist Lyudmila Savchuk worked there undercover for two months[24] – the account itself did not look particularly suspicious. Computers might struggle to fake human behavior perfectly (less so with the advent of large language models such as that driving ChatGPT), but humans are quite capable of this, and the Jenna Abrams account was managed by decidedly skilled humans. In fact, cases such as the Jenna Abrams one questions the very meaning itself of 'fake' on social platforms. Not releasing one's identity is a perfectly legitimate choice, as is having more than one account. Impersonating someone else's identity is not legitimate, but impersonating a fictional person presumably is. And what about accounts that *parody* important X personas?

When we talk about 'fake' accounts, we generally mean that they are *deceiving* about their true identity. But this is a subjective definition. There is nothing harmful in parody, anonymous, or even orchestrated pools of accounts as long as users are *aware* of what is going on behind the tweets they read.

Unfortunately, the typical level of awareness on how online social network are shaped, and on the dynamics of information flowing over them, is low — understandably so, because behind the simple and catchy interface, the networks themselves are huge and complicated. Basing one's opinion on information obtained via online social networks in which millions of users everyday share their — and their peers' — views is already a daunting task. But when a large part of these social networks are simply not what they seem – not the spontaneous activity of many fellow citizens, but rather a coordinated and well–organized program of deception led by teams of experts — then distinguishing true information from fake news, or even just honest debate from trolling, is simply impossible. Unless, that is, one has some *external* trusted sources against which to evaluate 'news from the crowd'. But it is a fact that a large proportion of citizens in Western democracies overwhelmingly access the news and make political decisions through online social networks.

Clearly, the presence of even a large number of fake accounts on online social platforms would not deserve the media attention it received in recent years, had such platforms not played such an integral role in the public debate. But the fact that fake nodes were able to blend so easily into the 'real' public opinion makes it evident that, if the staff at X and external researchers have trouble unmasking fake accounts, then ordinary users have no chance. And the clash between having an interlocutor at one's fingertips, communicating with her as if she was your friend, and having no idea of her actual identity is precisely what challenges the user's common sense.

We might not consider our close colleagues, family members, and friends distinguished experts in politics, but they still have a *reputation* to defend with us, which means that by trial and error we learn how much to trust them, and they learn that they must stand behind their statements if they want to be trusted. Moreover, we typically know something about their interests and sources of information, and we take this into account when weighing their opinions. *This* is the kind of social network in which we are used to interacting, and forming our opinions. On X, accounts are expendable, the only measure of 'reputation' typically being the number of followers a user has, which is in turn easily manipulated. In the last few years researchers have made progress toward understanding how we can be deceived simply by manipulating the networks around us.

4.5 Deceptive networks

The problem with confronting 'reputation–less' individuals, and hence the difficulty in asserting the trustworthiness of their opinions, is certainly not strictly limited to networks. But there are specific ways in which networks mislead the human brain when it attempts to aggregate information. By way of example, imagine that on your way to work one morning, while you travel to work one morning, you overhear somebody on the subway talking about Tracy Grassroot — a politician whose name is new to you — who has declared her intention to run in the next primary elections, for your chosen party. You have no idea of how viable this candidate is, but the passenger close to you says that she is a great politician. Once you reach your office, your colleague tells you about

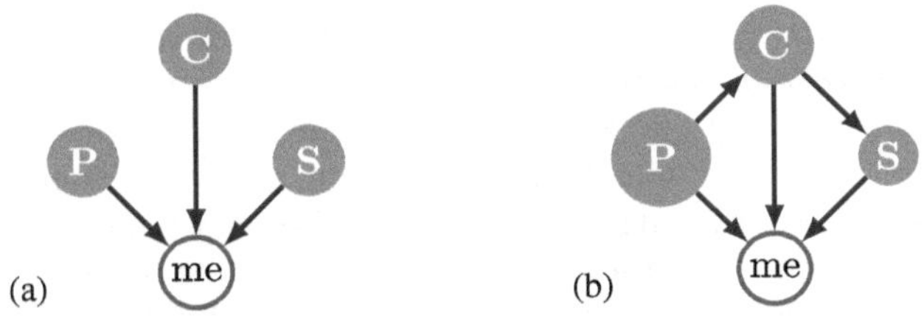

Figure 4.4 The perceived and actual networks including the Passenger, the Colleague, the Seller, and myself

that new candidate, Tracy Grassroot, who he has heard good things about. For lunch, you get a sandwich from the deli just below your office, and the seller tells you about that new candidate who really seems like the right person for the position, Tracy Grassroot. By this time, you might at least consider the fact that this candidate is *likely* to be a good one.

But would your opinion change if you knew that the subway passenger is a friend of your colleague, that they met just before the latter came into the office, and that it was the former who told him about Tracy Grassroot? And what if, in turn, your colleague had gone to get a sandwich just five minutes before you and told the seller about Tracy Grassroot then? In other words, what if the actual social network had the shape depicted in Figure 4.4b, rather than in Figure 4.4a? You might not conclude that Tracy Grassroot is a *bad* candidate, but you would likely laugh at the coincidence, view these three opinions with more skepticism, and maybe start looking for *factual*, or at least *independent*, information on the candidate. The social networks over which information flows are as relevant as the information itself — but we are not as diligent in questioning the networks.

Skepticism is a natural part of the way we assimilate information, and it plays an especially important role when the source of information is unknown. But abundant evidence suggests that when interacting online, where anonymity and straight deception abound, we tend to lower our barriers, rather than raise them. The structure of networks can influence the extent to which this happens.

Economists have long been optimistic about the so-called 'wisdom of the crowds', where aggregating the opinions of a large number of individuals can result in estimates that are as good as or even better than those of 'experts'. The classic example is 'Galton's ox': in 1906, when Francis Galton visited a fair, a contest was run where attendants were invited to guess the weight of an ox. Estimates varied, but ultimately the mean of the estimates made by the crowd was extremely close to the correct value — likely much more precise than even an expert's guess would have been — making a nice point in favor of democracy. A crucial element of the experiment is that members of the crowd were asked to state *their own*, independent estimates — not to discuss it among themselves and come up with a collective answer. In other words, the experiment resembled Figure 4.4a.

In 2003, economists Peter DeMarzo, Dimitri Vayanos and Jeffrey Zwiebel challenged this view by analyzing the phenomenon of *persuasion bias*.[25] They began by observing that the way in which societies typically discuss issues is not structured like the case of the ox — where everyone expresses the outcome of an individual reasoning and then the results are aggregated granting the same importance to each member's opinion — but rather as a network, where each one of us only listens to a selected number of other opinions and in turn expresses our own opinions to a selected number of listeners. Importantly, some people might be listened to by more people than others. So these individuals will eventually have more influence over other individuals, and not because they are better informed, but simply because more people listen to them (as in Figure 4.4b).

In other words, coming back to the example of Tracy Grassroot, I conclude she is a good candidate not because I have a high esteem of the subway passenger, but rather because as I update my opinion over time, I am unable to account for the *repetition of information*. This deceitful repetition is essentially what De Marzo and his coauthors refer to as persuasion bias. While listening to my colleague and to the sandwich seller, I do not realize I am still really listening to one source of information: that of a random subway passenger.

One might think that online social networks simplify my task of optimally aggregating information sources around me, because – in contrast to the example of the subway passenger — I am able to observe, to some extent, the structure of the network itself (that is, who follows who on X), and account for it. But in fact, DeMarzo and his colleagues found that this is '*extremely complicated*' even in small examples of toy social networks, and it only gets worse in large social networks, over long periods of time. And while, in real–life conversations, each side typically listens to what the other has to say, the X network of followers is directed, precisely like the one envisaged by DeMarzo and his colleagues (three years before X, then Twitter, was founded). So being heard by thousands of people is no guarantee of having a large number of information sources to confront.

Almost ten years after the persuasion bias hypothesis was proposed, Italian economists Luca Corazzini, Filippo Pavesi, Beatrice Petrovich and Luca Stanca put it to the test by running an actual experiment with human subjects.[26] The task was almost as simple as it could get: the network included only four participants, 'opinions' were just numbers, each participant started with a number, and the goal of each participant was to simply guess the average of the four initial numbers. Each participant would be able to see her network neighbors' previous guesses, and this was the mechanism that allowed 'opinions' to spread over the network. Despite the simplicity of the setup, the researchers systematically observed that if a subject 'spoke' to more peers, her opinion would be over–represented in the final guesses.

In fact, the analysis of DeMarzo and his coauthors goes beyond linking influence to the mere *degree*. Consider two 13–year–old classmates, Emma and David, whose only followers on Instagram are their own parents. Emma's parents only use their Instagram accounts to check what their child is doing online, and are only followed by each other. David's parents, instead, are two well known local politicians, each with thousands of followers. If Emma and David, walking together at sunset, each take and post a picture of the same brightly colored sky, guess who of the two is expected to get more likes. Influence does not just depend on indegree, but also on *centrality*.[27] In Figure 4.4b, the Passenger and the Colleague each have the same outdegree (2), but the Passenger has a larger social influence because he talks to the Colleague (and me), while the Colleague talks to the Seller (and me) who in turn only has an outdegree of 1. This idea, that one's importance depends not only on one's degree, but also on the importance of one's neighbors, is exactly the principle behind the PageRank algorithm described earlier in this book.

So the structure of the network over which information propagates is not a neutral element in determining how opinions are shaped. And anonymity only makes things worse. Because I have known them for a long time, I might be reasonably sure that the Colleague and the Seller would not lie or distort the truth. However, they might be unaware — because they do not know him personally — that the Passenger is not just any random subway commuter, but rather a member of the staff of Tracy Grassroot's campaign staff.

This depiction of social networks might seem overly pessimistic. Certainly, persuasion bias is possible, but maybe unlikely in real social networks, where we do not get information from just two people, but many more – in particular, on the internet. If a person follows hundreds of people on X or is friends with hundreds of people on Facebook, he has access to many more sources of information; while some of them might be affected by the repetition of information, one would hope it is unlikely that *most of them* are.

This might be the case if our connections in social networks were established randomly, but in reality, the opposite is true.

4.6 Truth, post–truth and customized truth

That the Facebook friendship network is not just random — or more precisely, that it exhibits strong clustering — is immediately evident to any Facebook user. The home page displays a frame titled 'People You May Know', which attempts to guess which profiles will receive a user's next friendship request. The feature might not be perfect, but according to anecdotal evidence it errs on the side of being *too smart* rather than too limited. The Facebook help page for the feature mentions four different sources of information (and dozens more were reported by Facebook spokespersons[28]), but '*having friends in common, or mutual friends [...] is the most common reason for suggestions*'. [29] Or, in other words 'Facebook exploits the fact that the network of friendship exhibits strong clustering'.

But the 'People You May Know' algorithm does not stop there, and also takes into account, among the pieces of information it uses, '*your networks (example: your school, university or work)*' — and many more, a list of which is not released. Or, in other words, 'Facebook exploits the fact that the network of friendship exhibits assortativity'.

Assortativity is sometimes referred to as *homophily*, a term of Greek origin that is defined as the tendency of individuals to associate and bond with similar others. Whether it is because people with similar tastes and values tend to congregate together, or because people who congregate together tend to influence each other's tastes and values, it is a fact that social networks (including online social networks) are typically strongly assortative. While this can be an asset for finding 'People You May Know' and for getting to know new people you may like, it is not necessarily conducive to accessing fresh information or forming a balanced and open view of political issues.

The strong assortativity of social networks results in what is often referred to as a 'filter bubble:' one's view of the world is reinforced, and even radicalized, by mostly interacting with like–minded people over networks that resemble Figure 1.10d. In fact, not only do we tend to hear only from people who acquire information from our same sources, but we also hear only from people who hear from us, creating an echo chamber that reinforces our opinions by making us feel that they are shared. This is worsened by the ability of search engines and online media to execute customized searches, presenting results that reflect what we have searched for in the past and thus what we apparently want to hear. This results, indeed, in a bubble fostering a feeling of being informed while actually begin isolated from facts and transparent information. Add to this the possibility that the bubble might also be populated by fake X and Facebook accounts, and suddenly democracy begins to look less like a pillar of civilization and more like a nightmare. That Facebook, X, and Google News allow users more immediate and affordable access to news than traditional media outlets is much less reassuring if these news sources are selected by users themselves.

These elements create a fertile ground for an opportunistic use of fake news. But even then, 'opportunistic' does not *necessarily* refer to Russian troll factories interfering with US elections because of the Kremlin's geopolitical interests.

Paul Horner, former lead writer for the website *National Report* and later the founder of the website *News Examiner* (both specializing in hoax news) produced a large number of fake articles, many of which ended up trending on Facebook and many of which he and other commentators believe provided important support for Trump's 2016 successful race to the White House. In March 2016, Eric Trump and Corey Lewandowski, son and campaign manager of the to–be US president, respectively, both tweeted a fake story by Horner reporting that protesters attempting to disrupt Trump rallies were being paid $ 3,500. However Horner was not a strategic member of the pro–Trump campaign: he stated in an interview that he hated Trump and even said, 'I didn't think it was possible for him to get elected president'.[30] Horner's motivations for the fake news were strictly financial: the large flows of visitors to his page brought in advertising revenues of reportedly $10,000 a day, at their peak.[31]) And in order to reach these large flows of visitors, Facebook was a crucial channel.

In response to critics, Facebook founder Mark Zuckerberg has multiple times reiterated the argument that the platform does not *generate* content and therefore has no duty to regulate or censor it. However, in light of several policy changes for regulating news, what emerges is more a difficult series of attempts to find a balance between accusations of conflict of interest (Facebook, too, profits from advertising accompanying the increased traffic generated by fake news) and accusations of censorship and manipulation.

In 2014, Facebook launched its Trending Topics feature, a service (available only to users in a small number of countries) run by a staff of journalists, who studied the list of most shared or liked news on the platform and kept only the authentic posts. In January 2015, Facebook introduced a system that supposedly would allow staff to suppress news flagged as fake from individual users' news feeds in addition to the Trending Topics bar.[32] But in May 2016 journalists in charge of filtering Trending Topics were accused of exhibiting bias in their selections, and as a consequence of the scandal, in August 2016, Facebook decided to replace them with an algorithm that automatically selected the trending news. The result was a surge of fake news in the section. Finally, in June 2018, Facebook decided to drop the Trending Topics feature altogether.

4.7 Safety nets

Indeed, the role of online social networks in relation to fake news is not clear cut. On one hand, being the main channel through which factually false information reaches millions of users, drastically altering democratic processes, is a responsibility that simply cannot be ignored by referring to them as 'mere platforms'. On the other hand, there are cases in which the line between fake and authentic news is blurred, and it is only natural to worry when a small number of anonymous individuals is charged with determining what millions of people will read. Despite most commentators — and fake news writer Paul Horner himself — claiming that fake news disproportionately aided in Trump's success, the president himself often claimed he was damaged by the diffusion of false information, even stating, in reference to *traditional* media, 'What you're seeing and what you're reading is not what's happening'.[33]

The solution is not an easy one, but that does not mean that there is no solution. In the 1990s, when Google surpassed all competing search engines by using its new PageRank sorting algorithm, the key to winning the race to the best user experience was to exploit — in an automatized, smart, and network-aware way — information produced by users themselves: the links that connect web pages among them. Analogously, social networks need new tools for network analysis that are simultaneously easy to interpret and difficult to manipulate.

What if, instead of the number of followers, X user pages exhibited the *centrality* of the user? This would immediately reduce the perceived prestige of those users who buy followers from bot farms, because fake users typically have a few or no followers outside of the population of other fake users managed by the same company. What if Facebook users who post clearly false news — determined as such by other users or third party independent fact checkers – were in turn automatically flagged as 'unreliable posters?' One obvious objection is that users would flag as fake all news that did not align with their own views. But assuming this happened, it would at least signal that those users were breaking out of their filter bubble. Moreover, users who flagged authentic stories as fake could in turn be flagged as unreliable themselves. The story of traditional media reveals that, in the long run, if information sources are not just expendable accounts, reputation becomes an asset they crave. Social networks might have too many sources for users to remember them all; therefore, associating each of them with a public 'credibility record' can help users make up their mind.

Possible solutions might be more complicated — or maybe simpler — but they certainly involve forms of network–inspired democracy that go beyond the mere 'one head, one vote' principle. What is often understated of platforms such as X and Facebook is the implicit reference they make to direct democracy, in multiple ways. Each X account is clearly decorated by its number of followers and likes. The same is true (despite past experiments in different directions) for Facebook posts. These numbers are naturally associated with importance, and authority; in other words, they are clearly interpreted as *vote* counts. But in a context in which accounts can be fake, anonymous, inactive, or extremely active, they should not be. Democracy simply cannot work if citizens can vote multiple times, without other citizens even being aware of it; this is why, in the context of any modern election, each voter's identity is checked against a list of eligible citizens. The 'one head, one vote' principle — which stands behind the number of likes and followers — is simply out of place in networks with expendable, and heterogeneously active, nodes. Indeed, in late 2019, Facebook for some time began hiding the number of likes received by posts (following a similar move by Instagram) — although assessing the popularity of a post was still relatively easy, because the lists of people who 'liked' remains available.[34]

It is useful to revisit Google's PageRank algorithm. Tasked with ranking web pages — typically expendable nodes — it does not consider each page, or each link to a page, equally important. But neither does it require a team of experts to *decide* which pages are important. Rather, it provides a rule to extract a democratic consensus from the network itself, while neutralizing at least some of the ways in which the network could be manipulated.

Again, determining what constitutes a 'fake' X account is not easy — let alone identifying them all. Instead, X and Facebook have all the tools required to identify users who have more influence in spreading fake news (possibly identified as such by third–party organizations devoted to fact checking, where staff have identities and put their reputation on the line) and reducing their visibility, or even flagging them. The real challenge is creating a system that is simultaneously robust and transparent: as long as the rules (including the exact methods determining the importance of accounts and content) are well documented, flagging users and content and assigning reputation rankings will be clearly distinguishable from arbitrary censorship.

Given the increasing importance of online platforms in democratic processes, the possibility of coordinating with national authorities on providing 'proof of existence' should also be considered. Users would still be able to use the network anonymously, or with a fictional identity, but those who decided to formally authenticate their accounts would be publicly recognized as such. Instead, as already mentioned, X has dropped the procedures that used to certificate the identities of at least accounts of 'public interest' (what this exactly meant was never clear). If the procedure was instead available to all users, and standard for those who tweet with their real identity, maybe one of Jenna Abrams's seventy thousand followers, or one of the journalists citing her, would have grown suspicious of the fact that she refused to verify her account. Verification could also come with positive externalities: for instance being followed by verified accounts could increase the reputation of those accounts whose owners decide to remain anonymous.

The 2018 Cambridge Analytica scandal, in which Facebook provided data about millions of users to a private company, was an important step for the public opinion of countries all around the world in recognizing that, now even more so than in the past, information is power and must be regulated. There is no reason why handing such power to a company whose business model is based on advertising should work. Discussion is a natural aspect of human society, but there is nothing intrinsically natural about discussion on online platforms designed by humans with very specific goals (maximizing advertising revenues) resulting in specific design choices. Therefore, we must ensure that such forms of information exchange do not devastate the ever–precarious democratic equilibrium of modern societies by putting in place a process of analysis and study.

State–of–the art data analysis should be used to understand how contagion is shaped, *before* it disrupts political elections. Is a candidate systematically supported by a large number of anonymous X accounts? Are there, inside the Facebook network, large communities where the diffusion of blatantly fake news is the norm? Is the entire network of X users in a country just not representative of the values and beliefs of the country's population? These research questions can, in principle, be answered almost in real time: independent researchers working on them should have open and easy access to the data they need from the platforms first — not because they are necessarily smarter, or more skilled than internal staff, but because the division of power is the foundation of modern democracy. As summarized by Carole Cadwalladr, the British journalist who uncovered the Cambridge Analytica scandal, '*this [...] is not about left or right, or Leave or Remain, or Trump or not. It's about whether it is actually possible to have a free and fair election ever again.*'[35]

The reactions to such crucial issues should determine the way in which large online platforms are structured and regulated. A user who has a large influence and exploits it to spread blatantly false news should *at the very least* be publicly identified as such. While most physical shops do not offer customers the ability to rate their purchases and user experience, eBay and Amazon, who often sell exactly the same kind of goods, do have feedback mechanisms. This is because their managers quickly came to understand that purchasing goods on the internet is not the same thing as purchasing goods from a shop. So if online platforms cheat our sense of truth and our instinct for sharing, their decision makers must also find instruments to cope with this — and politicians should ensure this happens, *before* it has devastating consequences.

If decision makers take this responsibility seriously, then there is some hope to also educate *users* on the importance of 'conscious sharing'. In particular, more *central* users, who play a more important role in propagating information of any kind, must be constantly reminded that with great power comes great responsibility.

Notes

1 https://businessinsider.com/psys-gangnam-style-hits-one-billion-views-2012-12
2 https://nytimes.com/2011/10/27/technology/personaltech/cashing-in-on-your-hit-youtube-video.html
3 Bakshy et al., 2011.
4 While retweets were not analyzed as such because the functionality was only added later to the platform, the approach of tracking the URL through the network of followers is more robust because it includes a larger variety of reactions than mere retweeting.
5 Goel, Watts, and Goldstein, 2012.
6 https://nytimes.com/2011/10/30/magazine/the-dangerous-politics-of-internet-humor-in-china.html
7 Shirer, 1990, p. 532.
8 Wheelis, 2002.
9 Harris, 2002.
10 https://bbc.com/news/world-africa-29256443
11 https://nytimes.com/2019/03/07/health/ebola-epidemic-congo.html
12 https://buzzfeednews.com/article/ryanhatesthis/china-is-arresting-people-for-spreading-rumors-online-about
13 Lazer et al., 2018.
14 https://thedailybeast.com/jenna-abrams-russias-clown-troll-princess-duped-the-mainstream-media-and-the-world
15 For research purposes, the tweets are still available at https://github.com/five thirtyeight/russian-troll-tweets/
16 https://washingtonpost.com/business/economy/twitter-finds-hundreds-of-accounts-tied-to-russian-operatives/2017/09/28/6cf26f7e-a484-11e7-ade1-76d061d56efa_story.html
17 http://dailymail.co.uk/news/article-5050169/Inside-Putin-s-fake-news-HQ-Moscow.html
18 Ratkiewicz et al., 2011.
19 https://nytimes.com/interactive/2018/01/27/technology/social-media-bots.html

20 https://nbcnews.com/tech/tech-news/exclusive-twitter-pulls-down-bot-network-pushing-pro-saudi-talking-n921871
21 https://nytimes.com/aponline/2018/07/17/technology/ap-us-tec-twitter-suspended-accounts.html
22 http://time.com/5337863/twitter-fake-accounts-bots-purge-celebrities
23 See note 20.
24 https://npr.org/sections/parallels/2018/03/15/594062887/some-russians-see-u-s-investigation-into-russian-election-meddling-as-a-soap-ope
25 DeMarzo, Vayanos, and Zwiebel, 2003.
26 Corazzini et al., 2012.
27 Specifically, in the simplified setup we are considering, eigenvector centrality.
28 https://gizmodo.com/facebook-figured-out-my-family-secrets-and-it-wont-tel-1797696163
29 https://facebook.com/help/163810437015615
30 https://washingtonpost.com/news/the-intersect/wp/2016/11/17/facebook-fake-news-writer-i-think-donald-trump-is-in-the-white-house-because-of-me
31 http://washingtonpost.com/news/the-intersect/wp/2014/10/21/this-is-not-an-interview-with-banksy/
32 https://newsroom.fb.com/news/2015/01/news-feed-fyi-showing-fewer-hoaxes/
33 https://bbc.com/news/av/world-us-canada-44959340/donald-trump-what-you-re-seeing-and-what-you-re-reading-is-not-what-s-happening
34 https://cnet.com/news/facebook-has-begun-hiding-likes
35 Carole Cadwalladr, TED2019, April 15, 2019, https://ted.com/talks/carole_cadwalladr_facebook_s_role_in_brexit_and_the_threat_to_democracy

Bibliography

Bakshy, Eytan et al. (2011). 'Everyone's an influencer: quantifying influence on twitter'. In: *Proceedings of the Fourth ACM International Conference on Web Search and Data Mining*. ACM, pp. 65–74.

Corazzini, Luca et al. (2012). 'Influential listeners: An experiment on persuasion bias in social networks'. In: *European Economic Review* 56.6, pp. 1276–1288.

DeMarzo, Peter M, Dimitri Vayanos, and Jeffrey Zwiebel (2003). 'Persuasion bias, social influence, and unidimensional opinions'. In: *The Quarterly Journal of Economics* 118.3, pp. 909–968.

Goel, Sharad, Duncan J Watts, and Daniel G Goldstein (2012). 'The structure of online diffusion networks'. In: *Proceedings of the 13th ACM Conference on Electronic Commerce*. ACM, pp. 623–638.

Harris, Sheldon H (2002). 'Factories of death: Japanese biological warfare, 1932-1945, and the American cover-up'. Psychology Press.

Lazer, David MJ et al. (2018). 'The science of fake news'. In: *Science* 359.6380, pp. 1094–1096.

Ratkiewicz, Jacob et al. (2011). 'Detecting and tracking political abuse in social media'. In: *Fifth International AAAI Conference on Weblogs and Social Media*.

Shirer, William L (1990). 'The rise and fall of the Third Reich: A history of Nazi Germany'. Simon and Schuster.

Wheelis, Mark (2002). 'Biological warfare at the 1346 siege of Caffa'. In: *Emerging Infectious Diseases* 8.9, p. 971.

5 Epidemics in finance

Co-written with Elena Sedano Varo

Markets are networks. When an individual buys a car, he is transferring money to a salesperson, who might then transfer that money to his landlord in the form of rent. In turn, the new car owner might later sell that car to his neighbor. Each of these market relationships can be viewed as an edge in a network where nodes correspond to market participants — be they individuals, companies, or public bodies — and edges to transactions.

But do we gain *any interesting insight* by examining a market as a network? It depends.

In principle, if a person is unable to buy the car he planned to buy, the consequences of that aborted purchase can flow through the network. The salesperson might not be able to pay the landlord his rent; without the rent money, the landlord might need to refrain from that planned furniture upgrade; and without the landlord's business, the furniture seller might be unable to buy that nice racing bike he was dreaming of. However, if another buyer steps in and buys the car in the original customer's place, these 'consequences' vanish.

Network concepts and methodologies are useful to researchers who study how markets develop. For instance, an important body of literature has developed on the study of international trade, a spatial network characterized by disassortativity (that is, countries with few commercial partners tend to trade with countries with many) and high clustering (that is, countries which trade among themselves tend to have commercial partners in common).[1] However, the fact that market participants are part of a network is quite often irrelevant to each individual participant. There are exceptions, related to disruptions of so called *global value chains* — paths that the production of goods take across the globe, before reaching the final consumer. So, for instance, the 2022 Russian invasion of Ukraine has made it temporarily difficult to source a series of goods and parts, from cars to the kaolinite employed in the production of ceramic, with firms scrambling to replace their suppliers suffering disruptions with alternative ones. But these effects were temporary and, again, exceptional: in normal times, the landlord does not care where the car salesperson got the money to pay his rent, and the car buyer likely does not care how the salesperson spends the money he makes from the sale.

DOI: 10.4324/9781003490951-5

There is one market, however, in which networks and network concepts are gaining more and more relevance not only for researchers but for market participants as well: the *financial* market. In such a market, the item of goods being traded is typically money, or, more precisely, the temporary availability of money — that is, credit. If you deposit your money into a bank account and the bank then lends it to an entrepreneur, who uses it to invest in a promising endeavor, that money is still *your money*, regardless of whether you are aware of it flowing through the financial network and financing this investment. If the investment fails, the bank might have trouble paying you back. The loss related to a bad investment, or the risk of such an eventuality, flows on financial networks from node to node, just like money does, only in the other direction, in a way that is crucial for market participants and regulators to understand.

In September 15, 2008, after 158 years in business, the investment bank Lehman Brothers filed for bankruptcy, due to losses of around $10 billion. While this number might sound enormous on its own — and rightly so since it is the largest bankruptcy in US history — the Standard & Poor's 500 Index, representing the value of the five hundred largest US companies, lost more than $10 *trillion* in the following two months, or one thousand times as much as Lehman Brothers alone, and the negative consequences of the crisis spread far beyond the United States. Today, the crisis is popularly known as the Great Recession, and it was the most severe financial crisis since the Great Depression of the 1930s.

There may never be a consensus on the exact causes (most notably, the large and generalized exposure to overpriced subprime mortgages) of the financial crisis, causes which certainly predate the Lehman Brothers bankruptcy. But there is overwhelming evidence, both from examining the abrupt fall in stock prices and studying accounts in the news from 2008, that the failure of one of the world's largest investment banks was an important trigger in the collapse of the stock market and had a pronounced and long lasting effect on global financial markets. Maybe the Lehman Brothers bankruptcy signaled the US government's willingness, or unwillingness in this case, to rescue financial firms in turmoil — that is, the news of the bankruptcy, rather than the bankruptcy itself, was mostly responsible for the stock market dive. But the one thing there is hardly any disagreement on is the fact that the unexpected and spectacular failure of Lehman Brothers was the trigger for the stock market crash.

This story has been told hundreds of times over the last decade or so, so much so that today it may sound perfectly natural. But is it really so obvious that a firm that finds itself in trouble (and possibly goes bankrupt) would cause *its competitors* to also face huge losses? Certainly trouble for an individual firm can be a *symptom* of trouble for an entire sector; after all, consumer tastes do change. For instance, typewriter producers lost their market to computers in a relatively short period of time; today, supermarkets and traditional retail stores struggle to compete with online retailers. But still, the failure of one supermarket or supermarket chain does not *cause* its close competitors to lose their market value; on the contrary, it can alleviate, at least temporarily, some of the competitive pressure. So one might have expected other investment banks to actually increase their profits in the immediate aftermath of the Lehman Brothers failure, or at least to enhance their prospects. This was definitely not the case: stocks of Goldman Sachs and Morgan Stanley (two of the firm's largest competitors) lost 30% and 40%, respectively, of their value in the three days after Lehman Brothers declared bankruptcy.

Examining the characteristics of financial networks can help explain why financial actors often succeed together, and fail together, and such examinations can be applied not only to the financial crisis of 2007–2008 but also to the dot-com bubble of 2000 and to many other financial bubbles throughout the course of history. *Coordination* is frequent in natural and social environments.

Analyses of the 2007 financial crisis often begin with the story of London's Millennium Bridge, connecting St Paul's Cathedral and the Tate Modern art gallery. On in its opening day back in 2000, the steel bridge started to wobble alarmingly from left to right. Engineers had obviously considered the weight of the crowd and also the energy that their steps would transfer to the bridge, but they based these calculations on the assumption that the pedestrians they would walk out of step. Instead, the crowd spontaneously coordinated their steps in response to small vibrations from the bridge itself.[2] This outstanding piece of engineering, designed to withstand the impact of a speedy 4,000-tonne boat, earned the nickname 'wobbly bridge' and was shut down for two years.

Coordination in the financial field works in a similar way. Take the example of bank runs, which occur when customers lose trust in their bank and start withdrawing their account balances out of fear that the bank will soon be unable to reimburse its customers. A bank run can be triggered by a negative shock, such as a bad investment, or merely bad news. The shock might be unimportant in the larger scheme of things, but if it strikes fear in some of the customers, they will immediately withdraw their funds, thus causing more serious liquidity problems for the bank and scaring more customers. The resulting vicious cycle, which can bring a bank to its knees, resembles the involuntarily coordinated reaction of pedestrians on the wobbly bridge.

The global nature of financial relations and the dependence of the modern economy on credit only add to the challenge of offsetting this diabolical feedback loop — particularly when instability affects the entire financial system, rather than just one bank. And just as engineers must take into account the possibility that the steps of the crowd may spontaneously coordinate, researchers and policymakers who study the financial system must take into account the tendency toward the spontaneous synchronization of market participants, giving rise to booms and busts. There is one further difficulty, however: while the Millennium Bridge was designed and built by engineers, the structure of the financial system primarily emerges from the interplay of the decisions of thousands of independent participants.

5.1 The origins of risk

The complexity of financial markets is not a recent creation of stressed and overpaid traders, spending countless days in front of computer monitors filled with numbers and charts. In fact, as researchers Alexander Lipton and Alex Pentland show, the roots of modern-day finance can be traced back to thousands of years ago.[3] Archaeological evidence suggests that as far back as 2,000 B.C., in wealthy Mesopotamia (present day Iraq), rings of silver were used by national and foreign merchants as a medium of exchange and store of value (as money is today). The story goes that foreign merchants would often decide not to carry home the bunch of silver they received in exchange for their merchandise because the heavy load would have impaired their homeward journey. They instead entered one of the temples in the cities of Ur or Uruk and asked the priest to keep the silver until the end of the harvest season, when they would return to the cities to buy grain nine months later. Meanwhile, *local farmers* were in urgent need of silver to buy seed and grow their crops.

The priest would hence use the merchants' silver stored in the temple to finance loans to the local farmers. He could only afford this operation because the temple's liabilities (the merchant's silver) had a longer time horizon than its credits (the farmer's loan), or in financial jargon, thanks to the specific *maturity structure* of his assets and liabilities. The farmers would use the silver to buy seeds, plant and harvest their crops, and repay the priest (with interest), *before* the merchants returned to reclaim their deposits. The very same principle is present in today's financial operations — and it plays a central role in liquidity crises.

In ancient Mesopotamia, ideally, the farmer would harvest the crops, sell the grain, and return the loan to the priest resulting in a win scenario for all parties involved: merchants avoid carrying their silver around, farmers can purchase seeds they desperately need with a small added cost (the interest), and the priest profits from the interest. In the end, the priest increases the overall productivity of the economy and the well–being of the entire society, simply by exploiting the maturity structure of his books.

But what if something unexpected happened during the long winter months? The farmer's harvest could be affected by weather conditions such as frost, drought, or flooding, and as a result he could fail in his obligation to repay the loan. Who would bear the burden of this loss — the priest, or the merchants? This is a dilemma regulators face every day: what is the optimal way to protect a society from the negative externalities that originate from credit operations in the form of *risk*? If a bank fails after engaging in reckless behavior, are its depositors expected to bear the losses?

It is reasonable to assume that priests in ancient Mesopotamia were aware of the risk of their operations. Should the merchant arrive before the farmer repaid the loan, the priest would likely be compelled to pay the balance from his own pocket. In fact, the operations by which priests in Ur and Uruk created wealth — both in terms of private gains and of total wealth of the economy —

were partly backed by their personal funds. Such funds allowed them to absorb some of the risk introduced by the financial operations described, but personal funds amounted to only a fraction of the silver rings lent to farmers. Today, the ability of a bank to hold less cash than liabilities is known as *fractional reserve banking*. In the case of the priest, this means that, at any moment in time, he is unable to repay the entirety of his debt (the amount of silver he will return to the merchant), and it is a consequence of the priest lending more than his personal funds are able to cover.

Now, imagine that the priest carried out a hundred lending operations, and crops failed due to that winter's dreadful weather conditions. The merchants' claims to recover their deposits (the temple's total liabilities, or total debt) could not be covered by the priest's reserves because the latter amount to only a fraction of the losses, thus leading to the bankruptcy of the temple. The likelihood of this scenario depends on three main elements: the probability that the merchants demand their money earlier than expected, the probability that the farmers return their loans later than expected (if ever), and the ratio between the total amount of debt and the priest's capital (a ratio known as *leverage* in financial terms).

The fractional reserve is sometimes described — and not just by conspiracy theorists — as a sort of magical device that 'duplicates' money, because the same amount can be registered both as the property of a foreign merchant, temporarily entrusted to a priest, and as the property of a priest, temporarily entrusted to a farmer. Viewing it as a form of *diffusion*, by which money flows over a financial network, it is easy to see that there is no actual creation of *wealth* in this operation itself – because the priest is a creditor of the farmer, but also a debtor of the merchant. In fact, the ability to lend part of the deposits is the *nature* itself, and not an incidental feature, of modern banking. Saying that fractional reserve banking *creates* money is a bit like saying that attaching a sprinkler hose to the tap *creates* water — just because it flows both through the supply network *and* through the sprinkler hose.

But consider the (largely hypothetical) situation in which a Babylonian priest, who has lent large amounts of money to farmers, wants to purchase a precious vase from another priest. He has no cash left, but in exchange for the vase, he can offer the credit of a few farmers to his colleague, or, in other words, make the other priest the farmers' new creditor in his place. If his colleague accepts, other priests from different temples might find this practice of swapping debtors as a medium of exchange very practical — possibly more so than moving silver rings around. They will have then *practically* transformed credit into money — that is, identified an item of goods that can be used as a standard medium of exchange. Importantly, this is an item of goods that they can freely create, simply by granting new loans. Does this 'money creation' make them wealthier? Not at all: their wealth would be completely unchanged if they continued to exchange silver rings. But this 'commercial bank money' — as it would be called in modern terms, as opposed to 'central bank money' — is an important aspect of financial systems.

In network terms, commercial bank money essentially amounts to the sum of the *degrees* (indifferently, indegrees or outdegrees) of nodes in the financial network. The (weighted) outdegree of a priest (his credits) adds to his wealth, and conversely, his (weighted) indegree (his debts) subtracts from it. A priest with large outdegree and indegree is not necessarily richer than a priest with smaller books; what ultimately determines wealth is the difference between the outdegree and the indegree. But at the same time, the case of Lehman Brothers illustrates that a node with many financial connections to other nodes (or, in other words, with a large degree) can become *systemically* important. The more credit relations it establishes, the more connected it becomes, and the more severe the consequences of its failure for all the players in the network.

Today, debt financing is critical to our economy, with businesses typically relying on financing from banks (or shadow banks, discussed below) in order to set, and keep, their production cycles in motion. For example, an automobile manufacturer will normally borrow capital to buy machinery, set up the production chain and pay workers' wages. In the last three decades, consumer access to debt has also increased significantly; for instance, the ratio of consumer and mortgage debts to personal income in the United States increased from 77% in 1990 to a peak of 125% in 2010.[4]

Indeed, the role of the financial system is to form a network that *connects* areas of the economy with abundant capital with areas where there are opportunities for investment. To say that banking, and the financial system in general, is a 'natural' component of a modern economy does not mean, however, that it 'naturally' works as desired. It is a complex mechanism that requires careful regulation and can cause considerable damage to the economy when it malfunctions. In turn, regulation must be based on access to reliable data on financial operations and positions and on state–of–the–art analysis in a field where 'state–of–the–art' changes frequently. But at their root, the problems of modern financial markets are not very different from the problems that Babylonian priests could face some four thousand years ago — they are simply more complex.

5.2 A contagious market

Chains of debt — where an entity owes money to another, which in turn owes money to another, and so on — are the norm in financial systems, and fractional banking serves as the prototypical example. These chains distinguish the financial system as quite a particular market and quite a particular network — one particularly prone to contagion.

It could be argued that chains of debt are not a specificity of financial markets. If a person lends his car to his neighbor, nothing prevents his neighbor from lending it in turn to his mother, who then could lend it to her neighbor, and so on. If the final user of the car damages it in an accident, the loss will 'propagate' back to the car's owner (or his insurance). But this debt chain contagion is more typical of money flows than of other kinds of goods, mainly due

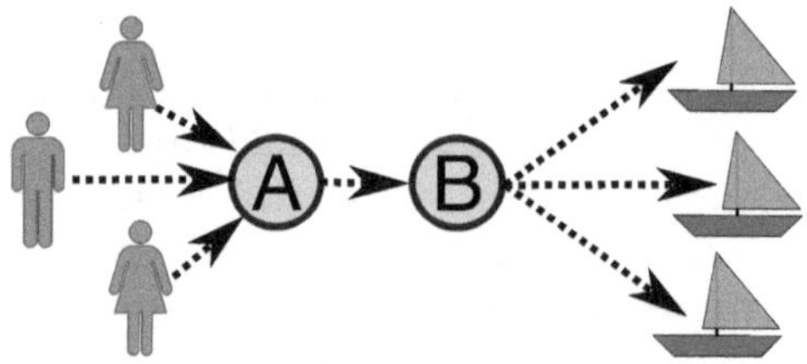

Figure 5.1 A simple network of credit

to the ease and cost–effectiveness of transferring money — even more so today, when it often only takes a click of a mouse or a tap on a touchscreen. Moreover, money can be used for many different purposes; when one person has no need of it for a period of time, there is virtually always someone else who is happy to borrow it (technically, money is said to be a *fungible* good).

Figure 5.1 represents a very simple network of debt: a number of private citizens lend money to Bank A (depositing it in their bank accounts), which lends money to Bank B, which in turn lends money to a number of firms in the shipbuilding industry. Arrows indicate the direction that money is flowing; if the arrows were reversed, they would indicate the direction in which a potential loss in the shipbuilding firms would propagate.

At some point, the managers of Bank B might notice that something is not quite right with *only* investing in the shipbuilding industry: it does not take an expert banker to know that investors should not put all their eggs in one basket — or, in financial terms, that investors should *diversify their portfolios*. So in order to avoid trouble if the shipbuilding industry faces solvency problems, the managers might decide to lend some money to another bank — say, Bank C, in Figure 5.2. The problem is that splitting the credit between the shipbuilding industry and Bank C, which happens to invest *exclusively in the same exact shipbuilding firms Bank B invests in*, only appears to diversify the investments of Bank B. Indeed, if these shipbuilding firms were to experience financial troubles, those troubles could negatively affect Bank B directly (in terms of deteriorated credits) *and* through the eventual bankruptcy of Bank C. That bank B is exposed to the shipbuilding industry's performance might seem obvious; that this also applies to bank A, despite it being at a larger (network) *distance* from the shipbuilding industry, is less obvious.

In order for Bank B to understand that the investment in Bank C is *not* reducing the riskiness of its portfolio, its managers (and regulators) should consider not only the direct exposure to the shipbuilding industry, but also the *paths* connecting it to the shipbuilding industry over the network of debt relations, and the weights of the edges along such paths. There is only one such path in Figure 5.2 — the one through Bank B — but in networks with more actors and larger degrees, the number can be much larger. Estimating the *total* vulnerability of a financial firm to a given sector or firm is possible and quite useful if we

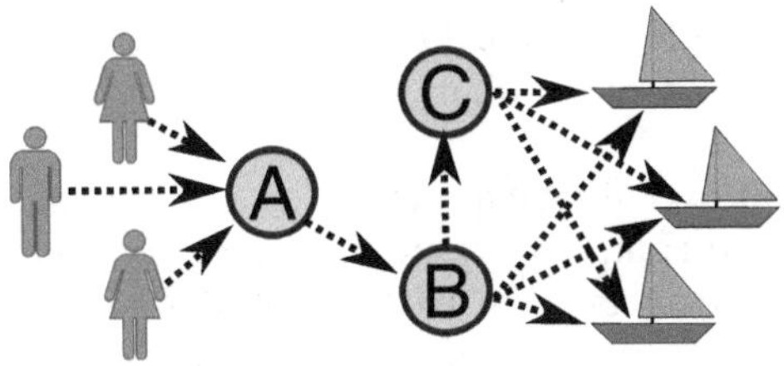

Figure 5.2 Bank A is connected to shipbuilding firms via two paths

adopt a network view of the financial system, but such efforts are futile if we only examine the edges to which a given bank is connected (its ego network). The problem is only exacerbated by the fact that, like in many social networks already encountered in this book, edges in financial networks are not placed randomly: rather, they feature strong clustering and assortativity. This means that a bank that tends to deal with shipbuilders is highly likely to be connected, in one way or another, to other banks that also tend to deal with shipbuilders.

5.3 The problem with expectations

Financial markets, like other networks, are subject to contagion: like a disease, financial distress passes from debtors to creditors, climbing back over chains of debt. However, from a network theory perspective, such contagion seems very different from that of a biological, or an online viral phenomenon.

If a person is infected by a disease that has a 50% probability of being passed to any person he interacts with face–to–face, the more people he meets, the more damage he will do. Similarly, if a user shares a fabricated story with her X contacts, the more contacts she has, the more misinformation she will spread. However, if someone faces a loss of $100 that he is unable to repay, and he distributes this loss among a number of people who lent him money, the total loss is still $100 — it does not depend on the number of creditors (or on the number of debtors, if there are any). In fact, the larger the number of creditors, the lower the loss for each of them should be (if 100 people lent him money and they share the loss equally, they will only lose $1 each).

Epidemiological contagion and the diffusion of fake news are similar to the diffusion of fire: if it comes into contact with flammable material, it spreads and grows. With regards to fractional reserve banking, money in a financial network is more similar to water in a supply network: the quantity of water flowing in the system corresponds to the quantity of water that was pumped in and does not magically increase just because the structure of the network changes. It would seem that the same can be said for financial distress: if $100 is lost by any node in the network, the loss might flow elsewhere in the form of unfulfilled debt relations, but the *total* loss should still amount to $100, right?

Wrong. For instance, as stated previously, the losses of Lehman Brothers — a single firm — were a crucial cause (although arguably not the only one) of a thousand times as many losses across global financial markets. The description of financial contagion presented so far can explain why distress *diffuses*, but not how it *multiplies*.

The problem of risk propagation over financial networks is exacerbated by the importance of *expectations*. Returning to Figure 5.2, some managers of Bank A might learn that Bank B is heavily exposed to the shipbuilding industry, and they might have heard of several firms in the shipbuilding industry facing financial troubles. As a precautionary measure, these managers may decide to close the credit line to Bank B as soon as possible (that is, as soon as current debt obligations expire). This will certainly worsen the position of Bank B, which, now with a reduced access to credit, will find it difficult to continue operating as usual — even if its debtors were actually financially sound. Bank B will need to minimize credit lines to shipbuilding firms it was lending to, and those firms will *now* be in actual trouble. Bank B can certainly look for other sources of credit, but other banks may conjecture that if Bank A has closed its credit line to Bank B, *there must be a reason*.

These examples are, on one hand, very simple, and, on the other hand, quite extreme — each bank has only a handful of debt relations, so their low portfolio diversification is obvious. But the mechanisms described played a crucial role in the *credit crunch* that characterized the financial crisis of 2007–2008, with firms, including financial firms, experiencing a general difficulty accessing credit: when you suspect that those seeking for a loan might go bankrupt the next day, you do not want to be the next tile in the domino chain reaction. And making a positive assessment of the solidity of the candidate debtor is much harder if it is part of a complex network of financial relations. Diversifying a portfolio is a difficult task in a network exhibiting high clustering.

Given the crucial role of subjective risk perception and expectations in contagion over financial networks, one might think that there is no chance of avoiding new episodes such as the financial crisis of 2007–2008. Certainly, a state can (and did, after the Lehman Brothers failure in 2008) help banks which face a risk of bankruptcy. But leaving aside the ethical concerns (should taxpayers pay for questionable investment choices made by highly paid managers?), how can the state change investors' *expectations* about the future performances of banks?

In fact, one could argue that in some cases, expectations are cheaper to 'fix' than the books.

Expectations played a central role in the *European debt crisis*, which started at the end of 2009. It began with the concern that, in a difficult economic phase, some European countries would be unable to repay their debt. Over time, it developed into a vicious cycle: the less trust there was in their solvency, the more interest rates increased, which worsened the economic conditions of concerned countries and, in turn, made it more difficult for them to repay and renew their debt – all while speculators profited.

The European Central Bank (ECB) put in place several large scale monetary measures to cool the crisis down. But a turning point in the crisis's development

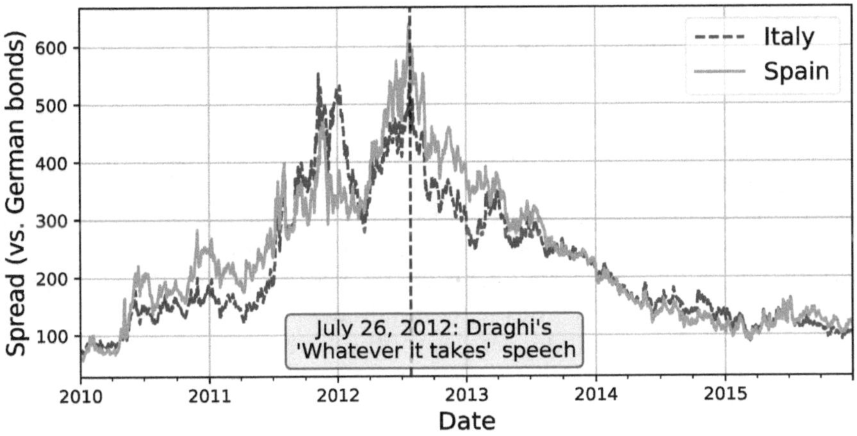

Figure 5.3 Spread between Italian/Spanish treasury bills and German ones

came with a speech by Mario Draghi, president of the ECB, who on July 26, 2012 stated: '*Within our mandate, the ECB is ready to do whatever it takes to preserve the Euro — and believe me, it will be enough*'. The extent to which Draghi anticipated the impact of his statement is unknown, but it is a matter of fact that the main indicators of the fragility of national accounts in the periphery of Europe (the infamous *spread* between interest rates on national treasury bills and the 'solid' German counterparts) reversed its trend on the exact same day as the speech, as shown in Figure 5.3. And while Draghi's words garnered attention in large part because he was at the head of the main institution deploying measures against the debt crisis (the Outright Monetary Transactions program of government–issued bond purchases was announced just a few weeks later), several earlier measures had already been deployed or publicly announced, but they had not succeeded in transforming the vicious cycle in a virtuous cycle — precisely what Draghi's speech accomplished.

The 'whatever it takes' speech was an extreme example of the power of shared beliefs. The speech included no *new* information on measures actually taken, but in general, information and communication are key to breaking the contagion of panic, not just because market participants receive news about the actual financial state of institutions, but also because each of them knows that other participants receive the same news. If an investor is optimistic about the future of the Euro, he might say so to his trading partners and contacts, eventually convincing them to be just as optimistic. But will this optimism spread in the financial network? He cannot know for sure, and he knows that if financial market participants remain pessimistic, the vicious cycle will persist. If, instead, *the president of the ECB* publicly states his optimism, the investor knows that *all* market participants hear this, including those at a distance of more than two from him, whom he might not know personally but who are linked to him by credit chains. Clearly, the viability of this mechanism depends on the *reputation* of the source of information, which in turn depends on the source's possession of reliable information about the financial market.

That financial regulators must possess data about financial markets might seem obvious: but in finance, information is money, and it is never disclosed *by chance*. Transport authorities can count cars passing on a particular road, health authorities can count patients admitted to hospitals, but financial authorities cannot just count dollars or euros flowing in a given bank account. Rules are needed to determine which financial operations, and which characteristics of owned assets, are to be reported to the authorities. Regulators need teams tasked with the study of the financial network, able to identify market players or areas that exhibit higher risk for the system as a whole.

5.4 Vicious cycles

Consider three amateur tennis players, Rafael, Roger and Jannik, who play together — two of them at a time. Sometimes, one of them has no money on hand to pay his half of the cost of the tennis court, and the other covers the cost for him — keeping an account of the debts. After years of play, Rafael owes Roger $500, Roger owes Jannik $470 and Jannik owes Rafael $450 — as illustrated in Figure 5.4.

But none of them is very rich — that is, none of them has cash ready to settle his debts. Moreover, the three never meet all together because Roger and Jannik always play on Saturdays and Rafael always works on Saturday.

Such a situation can also emerge in principle among the banks in Figure 5.2. In the same way that Bank B decided to diversify its portfolio by investing in Bank C, Bank C might decide to diversify its portfolio by investing *in Bank A*. The resulting financial network, represented in Figure 5.5 (omitting depositors and non financial firms for simplicity), might seem strange because Bank A lends money to Bank B, who lends money to Bank C, who lends money to Bank A. But there is nothing forbidden in it, and recall that banks do not necessarily observe the entire financial network around them when making their investment choices — all that appears in the books of the banks are the incomplete networks represented in the corresponding frames (the ego network of each bank).

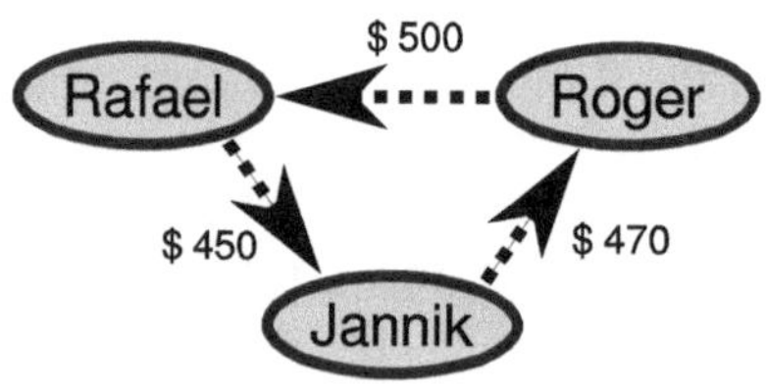

Figure 5.4 Three tennis players

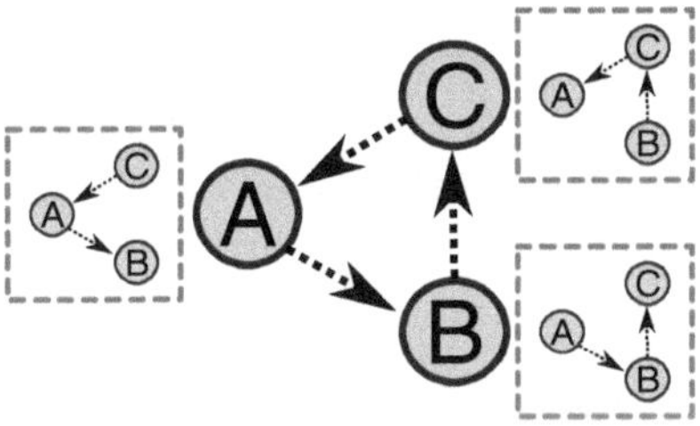

Figure 5.5 A loop in the credit network

As described by economists Tarik Roukny and Nobel Prize winner Joseph Stiglitz together with physicist Stefano Battiston,[5] this kind of cyclic structure can take the problem of expectations to its extreme. Assume that the three banks are connected through a cycle of important debt relations – to the extent that Bank A would go bankrupt if Bank B failed to reimburse the debt, Bank B would go bankrupt if Bank C failed to reimburse the debt, and Bank C would go bankrupt if Bank A failed to reimburse the debt. What if Adrian Adler, CEO of Bank A, had a hallucination, in which Bill Boston, CEO of Bank B, informed him that Bank B had gone bankrupt? Given the importance of Bank A's position in Bank B, Adrian Adler would file for bankruptcy right away. Upon hearing the news that Bank A filed for bankruptcy, Celine Chandler, CEO of Bank C, would have to file for bankruptcy too, and then Bank B would follow. At this point, Adler would realize that the chat with his friend Bill was only a hallucination, but in the meantime, Bank B (and in turn, Bank A and Bank C) had gone bankrupt in real life!

Obviously, real bank CEOs do not file for bankruptcy while hallucinating, but at the same time, real financial structures are much more complicated, including a multitude of market participants with widely different exposures both to actual shocks to the real economy (such as shipbuilding firms facing low demand) and to market *sentiment*, that is, the aggregate beliefs of market participants about bankruptcy risks. As strange as loops of debt may seem, they are a natural consequence of the fact that *clustering* is a pervasive feature of social networks. Recall that in order for a network to exhibit strong clustering, two nodes connected to a given node generally must be connected themselves; that is, the edges of the network form many *triangles*. And the loops we see in Figure 5.4 and Figure 5.5 are precisely triangles — which would be rare if edges were random, and are instead quite common in real social networks.

As already mentioned, an important difference between Adrian Adler and a real bank CEOs is that the latter will (presumably) avoid tying the fate of the bank to a single investment. But again, the example of Figure 5.2 makes clear that merely connecting different entities is not sufficient to really diversify risk, and that proper risk management within financial networks requires network methodologies.

5.5 Multiple layers of risk

In any network, it is important to recognize when nodes are connected by multiple kinds of relationships — that is, in a multiplex network. But in financial networks, taking these multiple kinds of connections into consideration becomes paramount.

Relations between financial actors traditionally fall under two categories: *debt* and *equity*. Buying the debt of a firm (typically in the form of bonds) means signing a contract — adding an edge in the network of financial relations — that guarantees a given amount of money back on some future date. For instance, I might buy the right to receive $100 back in two years, and pay $95 for that right with the $5 difference being the premium for my patience and for the risk I take (if, for instance, the firm enters a disastrous bankruptcy the following year). Alternatively, buying the equity of a firm (that is, its stock) means becoming an owner of a part of the firm. For instance, I might buy a share of some company at $100 today in the hope its value increases and I am able to sell it for $150 in the near future, but also knowing that I might have to sell it for much less if the company performs poorly.[6]

There are, however, myriad other types of financial contracts that are variations and combinations of these two basic forms, a complete classification of which is beyond the scope of this book. Today, the term 'derivative' can bring back vague but frightening memories of speculation and systemic risk, new challenges for financial stability and for regulation. But in fact, this term defines a vast family of financial contracts that are similar only in that their value depends on the market behavior of some *underlying* entity (which can, for instance, be a stock, or a bond); in reality, they may have little in common in terms of involved risk and potential gains.

Some financial instruments, such as Credit Default Swaps (CDSs), are blamed for playing an important role in the 2008 financial crisis.[7] Intuitively, CDSs are derivatives similar to an insurance contract, except you do not need to own the insured item, hence they allow you to bet *against* a particular company (similarly, one reason you cannot own an insurance policy on *your neighbor*'s house is because this would represent a strong incentive to set it on fire). Other financial instruments have been presented instead as a *cure* to financial distress, and ultimately systemic risk — for instance, 'CoCo bonds' ('COntingent COnvertible' bonds), which are discussed later in this chapter.

While derivatives, and complex financial instruments in general, are not necessarily 'bad', they certainly make financial markets *more difficult to understand* — for market players and ultimately for regulators, too. The difficulty lies both in studying how specific financial contracts will react to specific market conditions and in understanding how different types of derivatives interact in the same market. Similarly, it is one thing for an ethologist to study the mating behavior of gorillas, but it is another to predict what will happen to a pair of gorillas when put in a cage with a lizard, a tiger, a swarm of bees and an unspecified number of penguins.

Returning to the tennis players discussed earlier, consider the situation where Rafael owes Roger $500 but only if it rains tomorrow, Roger has promised Jannik $470 if Rafael loses his next tennis match, and Jannik has promised Rafael $450 if Roger goes bankrupt before next year. Nothing in these bets may qualify as 'bad', per se, but this financial network and the risks borne by each of the three participants are certainly more difficult to understand than the network where the only kind of financial relation is ordinary debt.

To make things more difficult, while most traded financial instruments are standard (for instance, any professional trader will immediately understand what a 'CDS on Google bonds' means), they are ultimately just contracts, which can be written *ad–hoc* by two agreeing parties. For example, the movie *The Big Short*, which provides enlightening glimpses into the 'human side' of the financial world, includes a sequence in which a fund manager (Christian Bale) meets the managers of several large banks and asks them to sell him CDSs on collateralized debt obligations (thus betting against the housing sector), by writing the contracts *ex novo* — because they were not available at the time.

Another way the financial market differs from most traditional markets is in the importance of *centralized* exchanges, and of *prices* over them. If a person wants to purchase a pair of shoes or a piece of furniture, she will likely begin by looking at the models and prices offered by several *sellers*. Depending on her location, habits, and tastes, this might mean taking a walk to the street near by, driving to the closest shopping mall, or searching on eBay or Amazon — in all cases, with the aim of looking for, and maybe comparing, offers from multiple shops. If instead a person is interested in buying Google stocks, she will typically look at the current price in platforms (stock exchanges) that automatically match mostly anonymous buyers and sellers, where participants can interchangeably assume the roles of buyer and seller, and where all sellers offer very close to the same price for exactly the same item of goods.[8] The price of a stock is hence simultaneously an important signal of how a company is performing, and an additional source of coordination for market participants: even if there is no formal relationship between them, two banks that have both bought stocks in the same shipbuilding company are somehow connected. For instance, if one bank sells the stocks, driving down their price, then the value of the other bank's portfolio will decrease as a consequence.

Financial networks are therefore multiplex networks where very different layers interact, and all layers contribute to the net positions of participants and to their exposure to different sources of risk. Luckily, compared to ethologists who study the mating behavior of gorillas, researchers in financial networks hold a powerful weapon: the behavior of derivatives can be precisely explained to *computers*. However, storing the description of a financial network is not the same thing as predicting its behavior and in particular its risk of meltdown. It is only the first step.

Characterizing how a financial network reacts to shocks is an intellectual challenge that has been tackled recently with advanced mathematical methods, and such characterizations are beginning to shape how economists and even regulators see financial markets. As seen in the discussion about Figure 5.5, sometimes even determining whether or not a particular bank, with its known financial relations, is bankrupt or not can be difficult — or, more precisely, multiple determinations are possible (either Banks A, B, and C are all bankrupt or none are bankrupt). But at least in that example it is reasonable to assume that all involved participants will prefer no bank to going bankrupt and hence there is no reason why (hallucinations aside) the banks should go bankrupt. Instead, computer scientists have shown that in financial networks which admit ordinary debt and CDSs as only forms of financial relations, even just determining the actual value of each financial actor's portfolio can become a very difficult problem.[9]

5.6 Risk taking and risk shifting

Thus far, we have examined the financial network — that is, the large and complex set of financial relations between banks, investment funds, hedge funds, and several other types of actors — as if it were created all at once, more or less by chance, resulting in each of its participants being assigned a specific amount of wealth and a set of financial positions. But clearly, the system of financial networks in the form we know it today was formed, and continuously evolves, based on the investment decisions and needs of individual market participants. And because some network topologies are more susceptible to contagion than others, one might *hope* that nodes of the network are typically smart enough to establish links that *decrease* their risk of getting involved in catastrophic failures. Unfortunately, if anything, the opposite is true.

Assume that Bank B in Figure 5.1 made poor investment decisions, lending money to shipbuilding companies that are unable to honor their debts. Its board has two options. First, they can admit the error, recognize that there is a problem, annoy stockholders, scare depositors, and worry regulators. Second, they can create a new financial entity (node) D, entirely owned by Bank B, and sell the problematic credits to the new entity D, as if they were high quality. Obviously, this will not *solve* the problem (the degraded credits are still there, and Bank B still owns D, and therefore still owns the credits), but in a world in which reputation is crucial, it might delay damages to reputation, and it might allow board members to accrue wages and bonuses for a few more quarters. Maybe later, more successful investments of Bank B will allow it to counterbalance losses, ultimately avoiding any alarm to investors. Or maybe Bank B will be able to sell shares of entity D to other banks, which are unaware they are buying degraded credits.

This example might seem naive: *clearly* the operation of transferring problematic credits to an ad hoc entity would not change the financial viability of Bank B in the eyes of a diligent, intelligent, and informed investor, or regulator. But real-life examples of financial engineering can be much more difficult to reconstruct: first, because of the sheer complexity of the actual network of

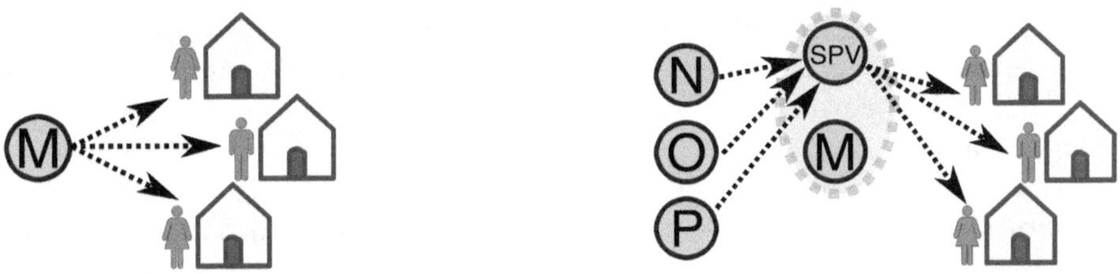

(a) Without securitization (b) With securitization

Figure 5.6 Example of securitization

financial transactions, and second, because not all operations/entities are subject to the same transparency requirements. What if, unlike Bank B, entity D had *no obligation* to make its books public to regulators, or to stock holders of Bank B? This would be possible if D had a different legal designation (being closer to retail customers, banks are regulated more strictly than investment funds, for instance), or because D was subject to a different national jurisdiction with less transparency requirements.

The reader might notice a similarity between the problem of shell companies and the problem of fake accounts on online social networks, analyzed in the previous chapter: in both cases, the expendability of nodes is a problem — which would not affect, for instance, the network of social contact analyzed in Chapter 3. Indeed, financial networks are a context — like the diffusion of fake news, and unlike the diffusion of epidemics — in which different actors have vastly different, often contrasting, interests. And these interests might include *hiding* parts of the financial network itself from each other — and from the regulators. In the case of X, identifying a number of accounts managed by Russian troll factories pertaining to a single entity was a crucial step in understanding what was happening; in the same way, regulators must be able to analyze banks and other financial entities by including their subsidiaries in the analysis — even entities (nodes) that are only partially controlled. Ultimately, reconstructing control relations between firms really requires a complete view of the network — and a 'network view' of the problem.

Unfortunately, given the complexity of the financial system, market participants themselves are not always entirely aware of the kind of risk they are managing – and neither does the regulator fully grasp what is going on. This uncertainty is magnified by the mechanism of *securitization*.

Consider a bank that has offered mortgages to several clients, who used them to buy houses, as in Figure 5.6a. The clients will take decades to repay their entire debt, and in the meantime, the bank is unable to use that capital to make further investments. What the bank can do instead, in order into a liquid investment, is create a 'Special Purpose Vehicle' (SPV) and transfer the credits to it (just like the priest would sell the farmers' credits to buy the precious vase). The SPV will then pool all the mortgages and sell the resulting security to other investors, as in Figure 5.6b.[10] What Banks N, O, and P will end up buying are *collateralized debt obligations* (CDOs — the 'collateralized' qualification meaning that, if homeowners fail to repay the loans, their houses can be taken as compensation).

The popularity of securitization capitalized on the idea that '*liabilities could be turned into bits of paper that you could sell to anyone*',[11] thus drawing immediate cash from a naturally illiquid investment (mortgages). *In principle*, it severs the transmission of risk from mortgages to the bank — because even though the SPV is controlled by the bank, its assets and liabilities do not appear on the bank's balance sheet. If the underlying pool of mortgages turns out to be *rotten* (or *subprime*), the loss will be borne by private investors, the buyers of the 'bits of paper'. It is, *in principle*, as if the bank had absolved its function of connecting the demand of credit with the supply of credit, and then detached itself from the network of credit — and from its risk for contagion. Everybody is happy, right? The new farmers (the homeowners) have their credit, the new merchants (Banks N, O, P) have supplied it, and the new priest (Bank M) bears no risk at all.

But risk does not just magically disappear. For Banks N, O, and P, buying CDOs is like buying a few mortgages — or, in principle, even better because many mortgages are bundled together, automatically 'differentiating' the risk. The problem is that the number of contracts underlying the CDOs makes it virtually impossible for them to actually *know* what (risk) they are buying. In other words, the CDO holders bear the same risk that the bank was bearing, but the number of potential 'chains of risk' in the network has exploded, and the counterpart that ultimately bears the risk has become less and less clear in the process. In the aftermath of the crisis of 2008, it is estimated that in order to truly be aware of the characteristics (the ultimate content) of some financial products (CDOs, for example), traders who bought them would have had to read *thousands of pages* of documentation, riddled with technicalities.[12]

We now know that the decline in lending standards rendered mortgage-backed securities close to valueless, but this was not evident at the time of the housing bubble escalation — neither to investors, nor apparently to credit rating agencies, which continued to assign CDOs good ratings. Between just 2005 and 2007, major US banks and Wall Street firms sold out somewhere near \$300 billion worth of CDOs, of which around \$240 billion were rated triple–A — that is, safe investments.[13] Due to the inextricable securitization process, assets with high default risks were treated as riskless for accounting purposes — the risk was there, but at a sufficient (network) distance that made it impossible for owners (or regulators) to see it. And apparently, not even the issuers of CDOs were themselves aware of what exactly they were selling, evidenced by the fact that traders at some banks deemed it reasonable to re–enter the game by buying their peers' CDOs (that is, not even Bank M was really safe). This is how the isolation between the conventional banking sector and the SPVs broke: the financial network was all connected, and it was all in trouble.

In the third quarter of 2007, Morgan Stanley's declared exposure to the CDO market was $10.4 billion.[14] When the housing bubble burst, nobody knew exactly how many eggs were in the real estate basket. Throughout the financial network, *panic* began to spread, not just mere losses. The latter spreads through edges of the network, but the former spreads when the edges of the network are not even really known or understood. And in 2008 we did not understand the distribution of risk throughout the financial market any better than Milan inhabitants understood the propagation of plague in 1630.

In the aftermath of the meltdown of 2008, the pages of newspapers were filled with reports about the large bonuses paid to managers of bailed out banks, the perverse incentives of rating agencies, and other problematic ethical and moral issues characterizing the financial sector. That is, features *of the single nodes* were emphasized, pointing out individual responsibilities for the disaster. And indeed, these factors (unlike 'poisoners' in Milan in 1630) may have played an important role and caused a great expense to governments — and ultimately taxpayers — all around the world who stepped in to save their financial institutions. But the financial troubles were at least in part due to risks that could have been taken in perfectly good faith.

Subprime mortgages — and CDOs based on them — are, as the acronym states, 'collateralized': if a homeowner fails to repay his mortgage, the creditor can always seize his house and sell it. Impoverished people get a chance to own a house, and investors are guaranteed not to lose their money if things turn bad. This win–win reasoning made perfect sense at the *individual* level, but multiplied by a large number of cases, and complicated by the complex and unknown paths in the network of credit, it ultimately first inflated and then burst a bubble in housing prices. This caused the actual value of collateral (houses) to fall, leaving people without houses, houses without people, and investors with losses.

So, although the fragility of financial networks can be worsened by unethical, or even unlawful, behavior, financial crises are compatible with the actions of honest and diligent practitioners who simply fail to account for the network around them. And unfortunately, one cannot just ask nodes (banks, for instance) to play it safe by acting in isolation — it is *their job* to create connections.

5.7 The job of regulators

Regulation is the way for modern legal systems to prevent negative externalities or generate compensation when such externalities cannot be avoided. The expectations — and *fear* — of contagion in financial networks make clear regulation and dissemination of information even more important.

Finance is global, as is the network of debt and credit. For this reason, since the late 1980s, an international committee of regulators — the Basel Committee for Banking Supervision (named after the Swiss city where it meets) — has issued standardized regulatory and capital requirements for banks worldwide

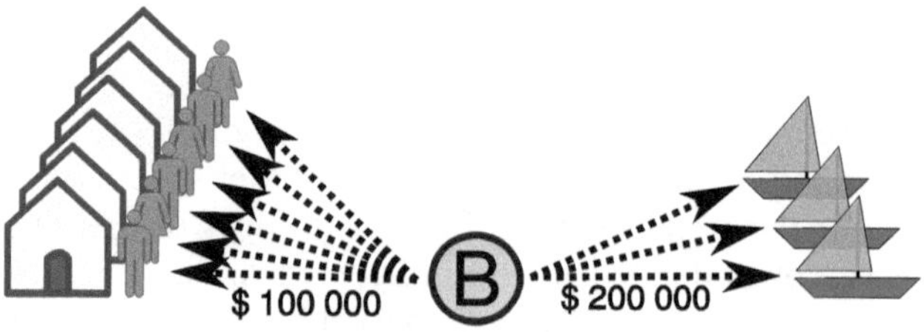

Figure 5.7 A bank lending to firms and to individuals

known today as the 'Basel III accords'. This third version of the accords, which followed two previous iterations, was rapidly put in place after the momentous events that took place in the financial crisis of 2007–2008, and includes reinforced capital requirements — meaning Babylonian priests must maintain more cash in their temples to compensate for the eventuality of insolvent farmers — and refined methods for asset prudent valuation — which means that, when estimating the value of farmers' credits, priests must account for the fact that some farmers will eventually become insolvent.

The principles behind Basel III accords are not particularly controversial. Increasing the capital requirements for banks can be compared to stating that people should get vaccinated. Basing these requirements on the state of owned assets — on financial connections — can be compared to stating that health workers, who are in contact with sick people, should *really* get vaccinated. The problem is defining 'the state of owned assets', because in financial networks, the risk of a node depends on the entire network.

Consider a bank that both offers mortgages to retail consumers and finances expansion plans for shipbuilding companies, as in Figure 5.7. In its portfolio, it might have one hundred mortgages for \$100,000 each, and fifty corporate loans for \$200,000 each. In other words, *in principle*, its portfolio is worth \$10 million in mortgages plus \$10 million in corporate loans for a total of \$20 million in credits (this is the *nominal* value). *In practice*, however, there are always some debtors who will be unable to repay their debt, and the probability that any single borrower fails to repay may depend on the type of borrower.

For instance, bank employees might know, from past experience, that 10% of mortgage owners and 30% of shipbuilding firms will, on average, be unable to repay their debts. They will then estimate the value of the portfolio by *discounting* the value of each of the two pools by the appropriate rate. So the value of the mortgage credits is only 90% of their nominal value (that is, \$9 million), and the value of the shipbuilding firms' credits is only 70% of their nominal value (that is, \$7 million), for a total expected value of the portfolio of \$16 million. This is called 'Risk Weighted Assets' (RWA), and it is a central element of the Basel III capital requirements.

The RWA is a simple combination of the nominal values of different positions with their probability of default. But while the former is uncontroversial, the real problem lies in the latter. As previously stated, the 10% and 30% default rates are estimated by bank officials based on *experience*, but this concept is quite vague. What guarantees that mortgage owners will fail at the same rate at which they have failed in the past? What if this bank has no previous experience financing shipbuilding firms? And most importantly, what if the debtor is not an individual or a shipbuilding firm, but another financial entity, with its own portfolio and its own exposure to risk (like Bank C could be for Bank B in Figure 5.2)?

The estimation of the probabilities of default of a bank's assets is ultimately delegated to the bank itself through its 'Internal Model Methods' (IMMs). These are methodologies — potentially very sophisticated — that estimate the risk intrinsic to specific assets.[15] An alternative approach to IMMs is to base the risk assessment on the credit ratings provided by credit rating agencies. But IMMs are generally preferred by banks — and maybe for good reason, given the credit agencies' limited ability to predict the 2007 financial crisis. Who better than a bank's staff should know the risk profile of its portfolio?

Unfortunately, on top of the objective difficulty of estimating the required probabilities, there is a problem of *moral hazard*: ultimately delegating the estimation of risk to banks themselves is a bit like saying there is a speed limit on a road, but that the speed limit is set by each car driver individually. A bank has all the interest to boost the books and give an overstated appearance of creditworthiness. Simulating a healthy financial state will allow the bank to borrow more easily in the capital market[16] and reduce the pressure of capital requirements. Moreover, board members receive bonuses based on the short-term performance of the bank, performance that can be embellished by 'cooking the books'.

To counteract bad incentives, IMM self–assessment methods must be approved by supervisory authorities, which look for flaws in the valuation of risk. Capital add–ons may be asked from banks to compensate for the overly positive outlook of their own financial position. For instance, in the Eurozone, this is done once a year by the European Central Bank under the so–called Supervisory Review and Evaluation Process (SREP). The SREP assessment considers qualitative and quantitative data (such as stress tests — more on this below) in order to evaluate the risk to which a bank is subject. In particular, for each bank analyzed, a Joint Supervisory Teams (JST) of a few inspectors (the number depending on the size of the bank) produces a report that assigns a score, from 1 (low risk) to 4 (high risk). But to what extent can this single number account for the complex financial network in which the bank can be integrated?

The example of an RWA presented previously was very simple, as the financial network was almost non-existent — the bank in question was only lending money to 'final consumers' of credit. As already mentioned, things get more complicated with non–trivial financial networks. Each JST's mission is to identify the *actual* composition of the credit portfolio — for instance, understanding the level to which Bank A in Figure 5.2 is actually exposed to the shipbuilding industry. This is done through a process called 'look–through', in which the JST components reconnect a financial asset — such as an investment in a fund — to its ultimate content — for instance, the loans made by such funds to the shipbuilding industry. In practice, the members of JSTs look at the most important assets and, when they represent substantial relations to other financial entities, 'unroll' the chains of debt.

The SREP also relies on so called — *stress tests*.[17] In simple terms, stress tests consist of simulating sectoral market breakdowns and calculating the impact that they would have on the market positions of the bank. For example, a stress test could assume that the shipbuilding industry faces a decrease in demand, combined with a recession affecting the country housing the bank's headquarters. The stress test simulates how such shocks may propagate to the bank's financial assets. But the limited scope of stress tests makes them ineffective in complex situations. For instance, when calculating the resilience of a bank, stress tests model the default of 'the two most vulnerable of their 10 largest counterparties',[18] discarding other possible transmission paths. And in complex networks, there can be an enormous number of transmission paths.

The Great Depression showed that the solidity of a bank can be threatened by a large number of small positions, possibly at a network distance larger than two — as the network distance can easily be increased by operations of mere financial engineering. Moreover, stress tests are not designed to cover a wide range of potential shocks. They assume a series of narrow hypothetical situations and test the response and resilience of a bank at a specific point in time.

5.8 In death of a bank

In June 2017, Spain's fourth–largest bank failed only a few months after having comfortably passed an ECB stress test.[19] In the decision declaring Banco Popular 'failing or likely to fail', the ECB argued that the breakdown was caused by the excessive deposit outflows, the speed at which liquidity was lost, and the inability to generate further liquidity. However, there are rumors indicating that Banco Popular had been dragging for a decade, the deficiencies that finally caused its collapse.[20]

It is difficult to say whether the smokescreen cast over supervisors could have been cleared by an enhanced stress test methodology that more systematically took into consideration the network of debt relations. Nevertheless, it appears obvious that either regulators were lacking important information on Banco Popular's book, or their models were not accounting properly for the financial connections between Banco Popular and other actors.

As had happened to UK bank Northern Rock just a couple of years before the Basel III accords were approved, and as would happen in 2023 to the US–based Silicon Valley Bank, depositors of Banco Popular began withdrawing money when they lost confidence in the bank's capacity to meet its liabilities. The reputation of Banco Popular plummeted after the publication of a report by Standard & Poor's in April 2017 which signaled the weak capitalization and deterioration of asset quality.

Unlike Northern Rock, however, Banco Popular had a weapon precisely conceived to fight such distress, in the form of €1,346,542,000 in CoCo bonds. CoCo bonds are like normal bonds but with an added clause that if the emitter faces financial distress — typically if its capital falls below a specified level — then they can automatically be converted into equity (shares), helping absorb the losses. For this reason, they have been presented as a life–saving financial instrument, and their issuance by banks has been encouraged through preferential tax treatment in many jurisdictions. Clearly, CoCo bonds are considered riskier than normal bonds, but holders are rewarded for the risk they take through higher premiums. CoCos were introduced after 2007 precisely to prevent capital shortfalls in the most delicate times — when capital is badly needed. In the case of Banco Popular, however, this possibility was not exerted until it was too late — that is, until the bank was declared 'failing or likely to fail' by EU authorities, and bought for €1 by its rival Banco Santander.[21] So neither Banco Popular's managers, nor its supervisor made use of the 'capital of last resort' to try to save the bank.

Why was the distressed capital of Banco Popular not boosted through CoCo conversion into shares *before* the situation got sour, in an attempt to avoid the default altogether? There is no obvious answer to this question, but certainly the fear of contagion has something to do with it. The CoCo conversion would not have *suppressed* the losses, as this was simply impossible. Rather, it would have *transferred* them along the financial network — to CoCo bonds holders, who were expected to bear precisely that risk. Despite conversion into 'capital of last resort' being the very function that the CoCos were conceived to solve, and despite the problem affecting (apparently) only a single Spanish bank that mostly operated nationally, competent authorities might have feared that exerting the conversion would have propagated the financial troubles — and fear of them — in the larger financial system.

The story of Banco Popular, on one hand, shows that the attention of the regulators to spillovers over financial networks has increased in the recent years; CoCos were conceived as shock absorbers, and ironically the decision itself not to convert them until the end was probably related to the desire to ward off the shock. On the other hand, it shows that the prevention tools at the disposal of regulators are still imperfect. Although CoCos at least succeeded in making private holders, not taxpayers, bear the losses, the result was still bitter, with aggrieved bond holders claiming that the intervention of the European supervisor undermined investor confidence and triggered a bank run.[22] A wave of legal actions followed.

This spectacular failure again reminds one of the peculiarity of contagion over financial networks: that money — and losses — do not just disappear. In epidemiological contagion and fake news, the deployment of the correct prevention measures — which can be vaccines in one case, and fact-checking in the other — will effectively neutralize the damage, preventing it from spreading further. Distress in financial networks is more similar to water flowing into a river in a flood: you cannot neutralize it, you can only try to channel it where it will produce less damage. If a bank has incurred important losses, someone — the stockholders, or the depositors, or some private bond holders, or the taxpayers — will have to bear the burden: there is no magic wand. Regulation, monitoring and intervention on behalf of authorities are important to understand the perils ex ante, reassure investors, and prevent panic from damaging *all* players in the system — and in particular, the most fragile ones, who are typically depositors.

5.9 Breaking the cycle

The clearest example of the importance of understanding the structure of financial networks is probably the phenomenon of *compression*. Recall the tennis players depicted in Figure 5.4. Rafael might be annoyed by the fact that Jannik has not given him back the $450, but he might also be ashamed of not being able to repay Roger his $500. and Roger have similar feelings about the situation. Enter Susy, who is a dear friend of all three, and to whom each of them confesses his financial troubles. Susy realizes there should be no trouble at all because the actual imbalances are quite small – once credits are taken into account, none of the three is seriously indebted. So she asks Rafael: 'Would you be willing to write off Jannik's debt of $ 450 if Roger accepted to write off $450 of your debt toward him?'. She then makes an analogous proposal to Jannik and Roger — each writing off $450 of outstanding credit in exchange for $450 of outstanding debt being written off. Each of the three friends wholeheartedly accepts this occasion to simultaneously recover (most of) their credits and settle (most of) their debts. Indeed, after Susy's intervention, Rafael only owes Roger $50, Roger only owes Jannik $20, and Jannik does not owe anything to anyone (see Figure 5.8a). This is the essence of *compression*; it operates in some

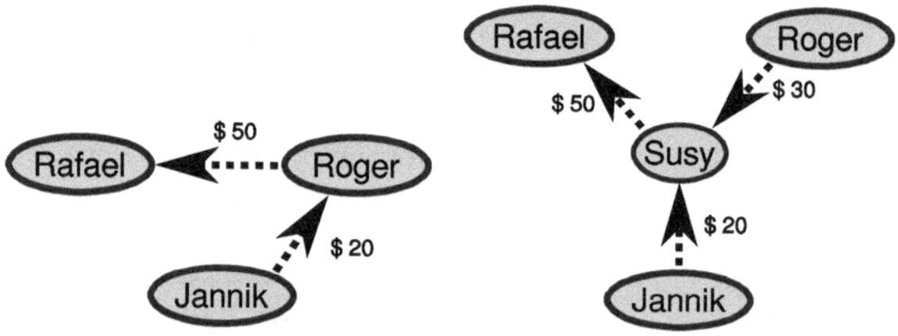

(a) After compression (b) Susy acting as CCP

Figure 5.8 Breaking the tennis players' cycle

sense in a direction opposite to fractional reserve banking, since it *reduces* nominal positions — by $1,350, in this case — by leaving the overall debt or credit position of each market participant unchanged.

Something similar has started happening in financial markets since the onset of the new millennium. The Swedish company TriOptima (now merged in Osttra) has proposed financial entities that operate in derivatives a *portfolio compression service* that finds *loops* in the network of derivatives positions and neutralizes them in order to help each of them reduce the total amount of nominal exposure. The task is more complicated than in the example with the tennis players because the network is much larger (TriOptima has served hundreds of customers, and loops can include much more than three nodes) and because the kind of financial relations involved are just 'debt', but a large set of different financial instruments. The results are also much more significant: TriOptima claims to have written off *$750 trillion* of exposures in the first few years of operation.

In network terms, portfolio compression decreases the outdegree and indegree of each involved participant by the same (large) amount — hence reducing the amount of commercial bank money (recall Section 5.1) — while leaving the difference between the two unchanged. That commercial bank money (sometimes referred to as *M2*) is *not* what we would typically think of as 'money' is evident from the fact that this significant decrease can actually translate into large *savings* for participants — not exactly what happens when you burn a banknote. The first obvious benefit of compression is the reduction in operational costs, simply due to the reduction in open positions (similar to how the tennis players were relieved by the intervention of Susy). But the main benefit is that leverage decreases, which immediately translates into easier compliance with Basel III directives.[23] And in fact, although the 'wealth' of each single bank does not immediately increase, or decrease, *some* of the risk in the system does disappear — for instance, because hallucinations of a bank CEO are no longer a risk for an entire chain of banks.

5.10 Shadow banking and the hidden markets

In Section 5.6 we mentioned the existence of edges in financial networks on which capital and risk can flow without regulatory oversight. Financial regulation is impeded by two pervasive hurdles or barriers, one existing between the regulated and non regulated activities, and the other being the jurisdictional domain delimited by national borders.[24]

The first type of border problem is well illustrated by the build-up to the 2007 crisis, when derivatives transactions were carried out in the dark due to their externalization to controlled entities. The existence of an SPV controlled by a given bank, for instance, might have been known to regulators monitoring the bank, but they did not have access to the actual balance sheet of the SPV (the edges connected to it). Stress tests such as those mentioned in Section 5.7 are hardly useful if a controlled SPV packed with derivatives is treated the same as a controlled shipbuilding company.

In the years leading up to 2007, when it was not obvious whether CDOs posed any systemic risk problem at all, disclosure requirements were close to nonexistent. Additionally, derivatives transactions were executed 'over–the–counter' (OTC), usually via dealers, rather than passing through a centralized exchange such as the New York Stock Exchange. In short, the structure of the financial network was completely unknown to everyone — and in particular, to regulators. It was a common belief that 'regulation of derivatives transactions that are privately negotiated by professionals is unnecessary' — in the words of former Federal Reserve Bank President Alan Greenspan.[25]

Today, years after the financial crisis, it is easy to place blame on this relaxed attitude of regulators. But precisely because derivatives transactions were carried out privately, and because of the complexity they introduce into financial markets, it was genuinely difficult to quantify and describe the risk they were accumulating in the system. In finance, as in every other aspect of our social behavior, the general legal principle of 'everything which is not forbidden is allowed' holds; moreover, it is difficult to draw a clear line between 'useful' and 'harmful' financial instruments. Furthermore, we must remember that financial regulators do not 'naturally' observe the financial network: information is released to them only if market participants are compelled to release it.

An important regulatory step was taken after the crisis, during the G20 Summit in Pittsburgh in 2009, when, the G20 leaders introduced the requirement to clear some derivatives contracts through *Central CounterParts* (CCPs). A CCP works a bit like Susy, or TriOptima, except that its role is not limited to suggesting to each party how to net out their position; it becomes a counterpart itself. Through a process called 'novation', an edge between a buyer and a seller is replaced by two edges with the CCP itself (see Figure 5.8b). As a consequence, whenever a single bank creates two opposite transactions with two different counterparts (for instance, buying CDOs from one bank and selling them to another), they will *automatically* net out, since both contracts are actually established with the CCP. It is as if Susy were now telling the tennis players, 'Rather than you paying for the tennis field, I will directly collect the money, pay for the tennis field, and keep track of your personal accounts'.

The obligation to recur to CCPs has dramatically lowered the recourse to services such as TriOptima's. When a complex network of financial relations is replaced with a star–like pattern around a single central node, loops automatically disappear — and with them, a large amount of notional outstanding positions. This might seem like a dirty trick, decreasing a *measure* of indebtedness without reducing actual indebtedness. But a reduction of the complexity of financial markets *is* a goal of any reasonable regulator, and ultimately financial players themselves benefit from it.

By taking on the traders' exposures, however, CCPs internalize risk and become systemically important institutions — just like the 'star researchers' mentioned in Chapter 1.[26] The consequences of the default of a CCP are yet to be seen.[27] Researchers are well aware that there is a tradeoff between a more dense financial network — where connections help banks diversify, and hence absorb, risk, but also help propagate risk — and a less dense one — where crises do not spread, but individual banks are more exposed to shocks.[28] At least superficially, CPPs seem to take the worst of the two worlds, as the density is low (small diversification), but everyone is closely connected to everyone else (through the CPP).

Shadow banking is another important regulatory barrier. This term describes the financial intermediation (including loans) offered by non-banks — hence, edges in financial networks that are unknown to banking supervisory authorities. The Financial Stability Board has estimated that in 2022, the shadow banking system (also referred to as non–banking financial intermediation) holds almost half of the world's financial assets, worth something like $218 trillion.[29] It is often in the interest of financial firms to avoid the regulatory category of banks in order to save compliance costs. And as everything which is not explicitly forbidden is allowed, there is no impediment to capitalize on regulatory loopholes in order to set up alternative financial enterprises. So alternatives to banks, such as peer–to–peer lending systems, have proliferated inasmuch as post–crisis financial regulation has increased worldwide.

The problems posed by this migration should now be evident. As mentioned in Section 5.7, banks are subject to capital requirements limiting their leverage. Shadow banking, and non regulated financial operations in general, escape these requirements, redirecting credit flows over parts of the financial network that are more obscure to regulators, increasing the opacity and complexity of finance and blurring awareness of its network topology.

Another way to dodge regulatory requirements is to escape the national jurisdiction of a country, the second important type of regulatory border.[30] The problem of national jurisdictions is well known in relation to tax evasion. While a company can register its headquarters in countries with low corporate taxes, it is assumed that the company will record profits and pay taxes for such profits in the country where they are effectively produced. But in the modern global financial system, the ease of mobility of capital across borders allows for operations that originate in one country to be formally performed in another. The Panama Papers, a leak of confidential records by the law firm Mossack Fonseca concerning 213,634 offshore companies, have proven that tax dumping is a common practice all over the world. Natural and legal persons systematically attribute operations to shell companies and trusts in tax havens, thus illegitimately escaping fiscal compliance. The problem is pervasive, with some estimates declaring that 8% of global wealth is held offshore. Not even the English monarchy has escaped the Panama Papers' scandal.[31]

In addition to favoring tax evasion schemes, national borders pose a serious threat to understanding the structure of the financial system. Even when available information is incomplete, however, network theory helps researchers go 'beyond distance 1'. This was done recently by researchers at the University of Amsterdam,[32] who analyzed offshore financial centers not based on anecdotal evidence or news from leaked documents, but 'simply' by aggregating available information on the global corporate ownership network[33] (98 million nodes connected by 71 million edges).

Adopting the parallelism between financial flows and hydraulic systems, the researchers identified not just the 'sinks' where capital flows, but also the 'conduits': five countries (the Netherlands, United Kingdom, Ireland, Singapore and Switzerland) that canalize offshore investments, effectively guaranteeing offshore financial centers a connection to the rest of the network. The method followed was relatively simple: the researchers identified all *ownership chains*, in which a company A owns a company B, which owns a company C, and they examined how often the company A, B, or C would sit in any given country. Now what is the problem if, say, an American company is owned by an Irish holding, which in turn is owned by another holding from Luxembourg? In principle, nothing. Except that the company will presumably claim that its gains are accrued in Luxembourg, and hence pay the very low tax rate of Luxembourg, rather than the higher American tax rate. And the real problem is that this behavior is *extremely* diffused (as opposed to, say, companies from Luxembourg being owned by American companies and paying the American tax rate). This is exactly what the researchers have identified: that the 'sinks' host a disproportionate amount of holding companies, and the 'conduits' a disproportionate amount of intermediaries.

Tax dumping is an extreme example of how easy it is for market participants to evade national rules, and of how difficult it is for regulators to coordinate their movements. But work by the Dutch researchers shows that network theory can help connect the dots (quite literally) of incomplete data. Looking for chains — that is, sequences of edges — in the network means transforming millions of pieces of ownership data into *patterns*, which teach us a lot about how and when the financial system functions, or malfunctions.

Notes

1 Serrano and Boguná, 2003.
2 'Explaining Why The Millennium Bridge Wobbled', *ScienceDaily*, November 3, 2005, https://sciencedaily.com/releases/2005/11/051103080801.htm.
3 Alexander Lipton and Alex Pentland, 'The Future of Money', *Scientific American*, December 15, 2017, https://scientificamerican.com/report/the-future-of-money1 For a historical account of the contractual and economic principles contained in the Code of Hammurabi, see Nagarajan, 2011. The Code of Hammurabi did not contain specific provisions relating to the principles that we set forth in the following paragraphs. Part of the description which follows of ancient Mesopotamian finance is the product of our speculation.
4 https://federalreserve.gov/econres/notes/feds-notes/household-debt-to-income-ratios-in-the-enhanced-financial-accounts-20180109.htm
5 Roukny, Battiston, and J. E. Stiglitz, 2018. As a side note, Stefano Battiston and the author of this book are not relatives — or at least, there is not sufficient data about genealogical networks to show they are.

6 The value of bonds and shares can also include the eligibility to *dividends*, and, in the case of voting shares, the possibility to exert control over corporate decision — but these aspects are less relevant to the present discussion.
7 J. Stiglitz, 2009.
8 Small differences in prices between different exchanges can exist but typically do not last very long because participants can 'arbitrage' — that is, buy and sell the same stock at the same time on two different exchanges — and make a profit doing so.
9 Schuldenzucker, Seuken, and Battiston, 2017.
10 The legal isolation of the SPV from the bank guarantees that investors really buy the mortgage credits, unaffected by the other activities and obligations of Bank M.
11 Lewis, 2011, p. 18.
12 We are leaving out of the discussion the existence of different *tranches* of CDOs in the same pool of contracts, which only adds to the complexity.
13 Lewis, 2011, p. 175.
14 https://morganstanley.com/content/dam/msdotcom/en/about-us-ir/pdf/Investor_Overview_2Q08_10Q_revisions_7-10-08.pdf
15 Ramirez, 2017.
16 Modigliani and Miller, 1958.
17 See, for example, European Banking Authority, EBA/GL/2014/13 Guidelines on common procedures and methodologies for the Supervisory Review and Evaluation Process (SREP) and supervisory stress testing, 19 July 2018.
18 European Banking Authority, 2023 EU-Wide Stress Test, Methodological Note, 21 July 2022.
19 Banco Popular Español passed the 2016 stress test with an ample Common Equity Tier 1 ratio of 13.45% in the baseline scenario. See '2016-EU-Wide-Stress-Test-Results.Pdf', accessed August 1, 2018, https://eba.europa.eu/documents/10180/1532819/2016-EU-wide-stress-test-Results.pdf
20 Gretchen Morgenson, 'Lessons From the Collapse of Banco Popular', The New York Times, December 22, 2017, sec. Business Day, https://nytimes.com/2017/06/23/business/lessons-from-the-collapse-of-banco-popular.html
21 https://ft.com/content/4cf8a400-4b4b-11e7-a3f4-c742b9791d43
22 See, for example, *Investors sue Brussels over Banco Popular sale*, The Financial Times, August 17, 2017. https://ft.com/content/b96003b4-8335-11e7-94e2-c5b903247afd
23 https://reuters.com/article/markets-credit/swaps-compression-to-combat-leverage-ratios-idUSL2N0GH0U020130816
24 Goodhart and Lastra, 2010.
25 FRB: Testimony, Greenspan — The Regulation of OTC Derivatives — July 24, 1998, accessed August 5, 2018, https://federalreserve.gov/boarddocs/testimony/1998/19980724.htm
26 Pirrong, 2011.
27 See the regulation for recovery and resolution of CCPs in Europe, https://eur-lex.europa.eu/legal-content/EN/TXT/?uri=CELEX%3A32021R0023
28 Elliott, Golub, and Jackson, 2014.
29 https://fsb.org/2023/12/global-monitoring-report-on-non-bank-financial-intermediation-2023/
30 Goodhart and Lastra, 2010.

31 The Independent, Offshore tax havens: How do they work? What can be done about them?, November 6, 2017, https://independent.co.uk/news/business/analysis-and-features/offshore-tax-havens-how-do-work-what-done-change-paradise-papers-panama-bermuda-caymans-turks-caicos-a8039916.html
32 Garcia-Bernardo et al., 2017; an analogous approach was followed by Loretz et al., 2017.
33 Chapelle and Szafarz, 2005.

Bibliography

Chapelle, Ariane and Ariane Szafarz (2005). 'Controlling firms through the majority voting rule'. In: *Physica A: Statistical Mechanics and Its Applications* 355.2, pp. 509–529.

Elliott, Matthew, Benjamin Golub, and Matthew O Jackson (2014). 'Financial networks and contagion'. In: *American Economic Review* 104.10, pp. 3115–3153.

Garcia-Bernardo, Javier et al. (2017). 'Uncovering offshore financial centers: Conduits and sinks in the global corporate ownership network'. In: *Scientific Reports* 7.1, p. 6246.

Goodhart, Charles AE and Rosa M Lastra (2010). 'Border problems'. In: *Journal of International Economic Law* 13.3, pp. 705–718.

Lewis, Michael (2011). 'The Big Short: Inside the Doomsday Machine'. New York: New Directions.

Loretz, Simon et al. (2017). 'Aggressive tax planning indicators: Final Report'. In: *European Commission Taxation Papers* 2017.71.

Modigliani, Franco and Merton H Miller (1958). 'The cost of capital, corporation finance and the theory of investment'. In: *The American Economic Review* 48.3, pp. 261–297.

Nagarajan, KV (2011). 'The Code of Hammurabi: an economic interpretation'. In: *International Journal of Business and Social Science* 2.8.

Pirrong, Craig (May 2011). 'The economics of central clearing: theory and practice'. In: *ISDA Discussion Papers Series*.

Ramirez, Juan (2017). 'Handbook of Basel III Capital: Enhancing Bank Capital in Practice'. New York: John Wiley & Sons.

Roukny, Tarik, Stefano Battiston, and Joseph E. Stiglitz (2018). 'Interconnectedness as a source of uncertainty in systemic risk'. In: *Journal of Financial Stability* 35, pp. 93–106. ISSN: 1572-3089.

Schuldenzucker, Steffen, Sven Seuken, and Stefano Battiston (2017). 'Finding Clearing Payments in Financial Networks with Credit Default Swaps is PPAD-complete'. In: *8th Innovations in Theoretical Computer Science Conference (ITCS 2017)*. Ed. by Christos H. Papadimitriou. Vol. 67. Leibniz International Proceedings in Informatics (LIPIcs). Dagstuhl, Germany: Schloss Dagstuhl–Leibniz-Zentrum fuer Informatik, 32:1–32:20. ISBN: 978-3-95977-029-3.

Serrano, Ma Angeles and Marián Boguná (2003). 'Topology of the world trade web'. In: *Physical Review E* 68.1, p. 015101.

Stiglitz, Joe (2009). *Interpreting the Causes of The Great Recession of 2008*. Speech held at the BIS conference.

6 Network responsibility

We do not need network theory to determine that vaccines are important tools in preventing the spread of contagious diseases, that a healthy dose of skepticism is useful when discussing news with friends, and that asset managers must wisely evaluate investments they make. But all human beings, and their enterprises, are fallible, and by employing network theory, we can minimize the social harm caused by such failures — because the risk associated with a non vaccinated individual, a hasty (or malicious) X user, and a careless bank director, strongly depends on the *position* inside a network, and on the adoption of policies that prevent contagion.

The position (and, in particular, the *centrality*) of a node in a network, however, cannot often be controlled by the node itself. X is the extreme example, because no authorization is required to become a follower of a user, and even less to retweet what that user posts. But even in the network of physical contact, or in financial networks, having control of a node's ego network — that is, of *direct* connections — does not guarantee control, or even knowledge, of its centrality in the network.

Everywhere there is a network, and phenomena of contagion over it, the *consequences* of an individual's decisions, actions, and omissions depend on the connections between that individual and other nodes, which in turn depend on the (past and future) decisions of other individuals. As inspiringly written by Martin Luther King Jr. in his 1963 *Letter from the Birmingham Jail*, *'We are tied together in the single garment of destiny, caught in an inescapable network of mutuality. And whatever affects one directly affects all indirectly'*. Maybe an X user only intended to share silly jokes with close friends when he initially registered his account; but if he happens to amass hundreds of thousands of followers over the course of his account's life, he will then need to be more careful about what he writes.

In contrast, legal systems all around the world are deeply rooted in the principle that an individual is held accountable only for his or her actions, not necessarily the broader impacts of those actions. Everyone has duties and rights, but such duties and rights do not depend on what their neighbor does or on their neighbor's opinion of them. There are some things users are not

DOI: 10.4324/9781003490951-6

free to write in a tweet — the typical example being anything legally considered defamation of someone else's character — but they do not depend on the number of followers the user has, or the number of followers the user's followers have. In practice, this means that the realms of allowed and forbidden acts are decoupled from their actual negative (or positive) consequences.

There are, admittedly, some established exceptions to this principle. Antitrust regulation, for instance, might forbid a market leader from buying a competing firm if the remaining competitors are weak — while the merger would be allowed if the remaining competitors held a sizable market share. The merger is not forbidden because it is wrong *per se*, but because the other competitors are not competitive enough, meaning, in some sense, the blocked merger is the fault of the remaining competitors themselves. In this way, antitrust laws can make a firm pay for circumstances it did not necessarily cause. However, these are exceptions, which typically do not apply to the rights and duties of 'ordinary' citizens, but only to large market players.

In the diffusion of epidemics, fake news, and even financial crises, *every* network member has a smaller or larger 'network responsibility' — the possibility to harm other members of the network. Since laws should aim to improve the well–being of citizens in a society, this discrepancy between the social nature of contagion and the individual nature of rights and duties is problematic. The traditional legal paradigm is almost powerless against the consequences of modern forms of contagion.[1]

Today, researchers and, to some extent, regulators are aware that fighting contagion over networks *requires* a network approach. But sadly, in most cases this was a lesson learned too late and implemented in a non–systematic way. Health workers involved in the Ebola epidemic of 2013 were eventually provided protective suits, but only after they served as a decisive vector for the diffusion of the disease. Concerns about the potential misleading effects of online social network platforms have recently garnered attention in public discourse and mainstream news outlets, but only *after* the impacts on the 2016 US political elections and the Brexit referendum were exposed. Both the Basel III accords and increased interest in research about financial networks were the *consequences* of the 2007 financial crisis.

In order to be more proactive, society must employ a systematic approach to network–inspired regulation, composed of three fundamental elements: the ex ante awareness of possible transmission channels, the ability to gather relevant data, and a system of rules that applies the insights from such analysis, and dynamically adjusts to new data.

6.1 Awareness

On October 24, 2008, most of the global economy was still suffering from the most immediate and violent effects of the financial crisis. In particular, the European car industry had seen a dramatic decline in value since the beginning of the year (see Figure 6.1). Then, between October 24 and October 28,

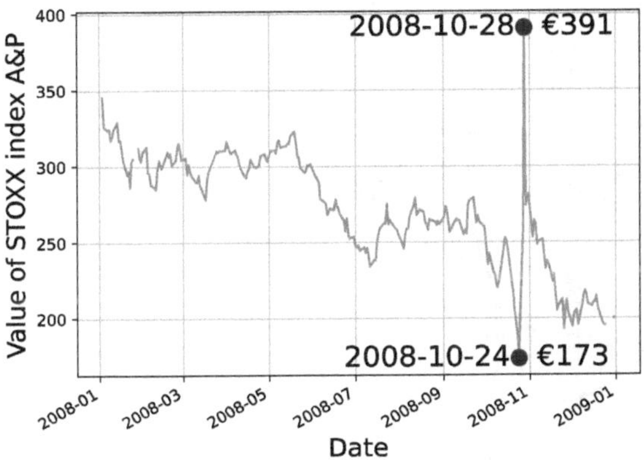

Figure 6.1 Value of the STOXX Europe 600 Automobiles & Parts Index in 2008

the index that measures the value of European automotive producers rose from €173 to €390 — primarily because stocks of a single producer, Volkswagen, rose by more than 300%. What exceptional discovery or exciting new product had caused such a surge in the company's stock, particularly in what can be described euphemistically as a poor–performing automobile market? In fact, there was no innovation or breakthrough on Volkswagen's part, and the increase could hardly be attributed to Volkswagen at all; instead, Porsche had revealed, all of a sudden, that it owned a majority of Volkswagen shares.[2] At least in some sense.

Listed firms of Volkswagen's size are not bought 'all of a sudden': on one hand, because the market monitors the market operations of big players, and the price of a stock increases in reaction to interest in that stock; on the other hand, because there are rules compelling companies to make their acquisition plans public and subject to approval of antitrust regulators. So how was Porsche able to execute its operation in secrecy, and ultimately produce enormous gains? Simple: it had not really bought *shares* of Volkswagen, but rather *options* — that is, financial derivatives that gave Porsche the *right to buy* shares of Volkswagen at an agreed price. Since the total amount of these options was very large, and the actual availability of Volkswagen shares on the market was very limited, such shares suddenly became a very precious asset, and their price skyrocketed. Volkswagen and Porsche did eventually merge a few years later.

One can applaud Porsche managers for their cleverness, but this does not alleviate a sneaking feeling of unease: they were able to carry out a huge market operation, which should have been, in principle, subject to regulatory approval, but they did so without raising even the slightest suspicion from regulators — and at the same time, without formally breaking a single law.

In fact, the cross–ownership network can hide surprises even without the intricacy of derivatives.[3] Consider two car producers, Alpha Cars and Beta Motors, each holding a relevant market share. A 51% of Beta Motors' stock

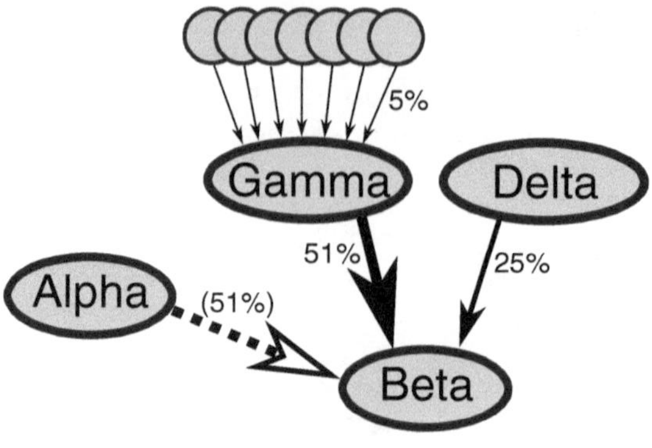

Figure 6.2 Example of cross–ownership network

is owned by the company Gamma Holding, and Alpha Cars is interested in buying those stocks (as in Figure 6.2, where solid arrows denote current stock holdings and dotted arrows denote the intention of Alpha Cars to acquire control of Beta Motors) in order to gain a monopolistic position in the market. For this very same reason, antitrust authorities will not allow this transaction to occur. But what if Alpha Cars instead bought enough shares *of Gamma Holding* to gain control of it? Alpha Cars would have then indirectly gained control of Beta Motors without directly buying its shares.

Presumably regulators are not so naive as to allow such an operation to go unnoticed. But the same goal — controlling Beta Motors — can be reached in a number of different ways. For instance, if a third firm, Delta Inc., owns 25% of Beta Motors, then Alpha Cars, by buying 51% of shares of Delta Inc. and 26% of shares of Beta Motors, would again gain control of 51% of the Beta Motors' stock. Or if the ownership of Gamma Holding is spread among several smaller firms, each owning 5% of its stock, Alpha Cars can secure control of Beta Motors by simply buying the majority of stock in eleven of them. These examples might seem unrealistic, but they also are not overly suspicious either. The network of corporate control has been shown by Vitali, Glattfelder, and S. Battiston, 2011 to be dense and control extremely concentrated. Determining who has control of a given firm *is* a potentially complicated network problem, and the high clustering of the network of control only makes 'workarounds' such as those described above more plausible.

Another regulatory issue that immediately involves networks is that of trade barriers and import tariffs. If, in order to foster domestic production, Country A decides to impose tariffs on apples imported from Country B, it should also make sure that there is no tariffs–free path going through country C by which the same apples could be imported freely. Similar arguments can apply to the movement of persons and capital across national borders: when imposing or lifting barriers, a country must always consider the other possible indirect paths. For instance, the European Single Market, which allows goods, capital, and persons to move freely across twenty–eight member states, makes them akin to a *single node* in any discussion related to protectionism.

In response to the COVID–19 outbreak in China at the end of 2019, on January 31, 2020 the Italian government decided to block all incoming flights from China. This was an attempt to stop the virus from reaching Italy, but according to several experts, including experts from the OMS and the European Union, this policy backfired. Travelers from China who were determined to reach Italy, in large part Italian residents of Chinese descent who had traveled to their hometowns for the Chinese New Year, were able to reach their destination simply by taking a flight to any other European airport and then flying from there to Italy. Ultimately, the measure had a limited effect in preventing travel. On the other hand, it made it impossible for Italian authorities to systematically check incoming passengers from infected areas for signs of the disease, and to record and track such passengers in the following days. The lesson from this policy failure is not that blocking flows of people is generally good or bad; it is that any barrier to free movement should simultaneously be enacted by any countries between which there is freedom of movement. The absence of internal barriers necessarily requires a joint management of external barriers. But such a lesson was not learned: on March 11, President Trump, also motivated by the spread of COVID–19, restricted air travel to the US from much of Europe. The UK was, however, excluded from the ban until March 14 (when it was included because of a spike in cases). In that span of time, traveling from France or Germany to the US was as difficult as booking a flight to London and then one to New York — something that many travelers do anyway when there is no global pandemic

A similar argument applies generally to security screening. At a given airport, passengers departing for many different destinations are typically screened at the same control point — and in some cases, passengers who take connecting flights are not rescreened, remaining in so–called 'sterile' areas of the airport. This effectively creates network paths in which the actual level of security is that of the least secure airport.

We know the prevention of contagious diseases requires awareness on their modes of diffusion, and this includes understanding the characteristics of transmission paths, and of nodes. The same applies to virtually any other relevant social network, including those whose edges can take multiple, sometimes hidden, forms. Policymakers must be aware of the different ways in which firms, users of social networks, countries, industrial sectors, and professionals can influence each other: because this will allow them to pass the best regulations; because this will prepare them to intervene when things go awry; and because letting citizens *know* that institutions are on the right page is the most effective way to prevent collective crises of panic.

6.2 Data is a policymaker's best friend

Once policymakers are aware of the possible relevant relationships between nodes of a given network, they must next collect the data required to understand the network's features. The need for evidence–based policymaking is clearly not specific to network–related regulatory issues, but the collection of network data can present particular challenges.

First and foremost, many networks of interest — including the trade network, financial networks, the network of social contact, online social networks, and more — are global in nature, meaning many different international governments and authorities must coordinate the collection of evidence relating to a network's characteristics and functioning. A successful example of cooperation is the European Systemic Risk Board (ESRB), which is tasked with overseeing the stability of the European Union financial system. Precisely because the financial systems of the different member countries are strongly interconnected, systemic risk can not be dealt with at the national level, thus necessitating the creation of an independent body of the European Union.

The ESRB has access to the derivatives transactions (network) data of EU market players, which they are now required to disclose to authorities, and ESRB researchers process such data daily, utilizing state–of–the–art network methodologies. Beyond the conceptual challenges, the sheer amount of data, which exceeds one terabyte per day, makes this analysis rather difficult, but standardization can help. The description of each transaction now includes the involved parties' Legal Entity Identifier (LEI): a twenty–digit code that uniquely identifies each node in the network. At the same time, an International Securities Identification Number (ISIN) is assigned to each financial instrument (or, in other words, the layers of the multilayer network), and therefore to each edge. Together, these standards mean that researchers at the ESRB and similar agencies around the globe do not need to spend time interpreting the parties' names and detailed descriptions of financial instruments in order to reconstruct the network of contracts: moreover, it is much easier for them to share data and results.

Another difficulty inherent in the collection of network data is related to privacy. Privacy is a potential problem whenever data about human behavior is collected, but public entities have several standard processes for anonymizing data at their disposal. For example, a revenue agency can provide researchers with a data set in which incomes and other tax–related information are reported, but not the identities of taxpayers themselves. The agency could also provide researchers with a random sample of the data set, large enough to allow them to run statistical analyses but not covering the entire population. Or, as a last resort, the agency could group observations in *clusters* of similar types of taxpayers, where researchers do not see the reported income of specific individuals but only the average of, say, the 0.1% richest individuals, then of the following 0.1%, and so on, splitting the population into one thousand small groups and providing aggregate information about each of them.

Unfortunately, none of these approaches works very well with network data. 'Unlabeled' nodes are not a guarantee of anonymity: if the shape of the network of relationships around the nodes known, it is often easy to reconstruct identities. Limiting the analysis to random subsamples means changing the network properties (such as average distance, clustering measures, and so forth), and the same can be said of aggregation into clusters.

Despite these obstacles, access to high quality data is of paramount importance to researchers and policymakers. Ironically, today enormous amounts of sensitive data are owned by private firms — recent examples being the new personal genomics companies, such as 23andMe, as well as *location data companies*, which collect movements of users who install given apps.[4] but also older companies, such as Facebook, already known for inappropriately utilizing users' personal data (recall the Cambridge Analytica scandal). At the same time, independent researchers and public entities have very limited access to such data, thereby limiting their abilities to study and address issues relating to online social networks and the personal data of individual citizens. Making user information and logs public is clearly not an option (as AOL learned in 2006 when it intentionally published, and then quickly withdrew the search logs of thousands of anonymized users, including some who were quickly identified[5]), but a stronger collaboration with authorities and trusted research institutes is a greatly needed.

These recommendations may not seem particularly novel; after all, governments have always collected information on demographics, migration, market activity, health, schooling, and many other aspects of society in order to monitor their regular functioning and detect any aspects requiring intervention. Meanwhile, researchers have learned to extract policy–relevant conclusions from such information. Most countries today have one or more institutes devoted to the collection and analysis of national data, and many of these institutes have decades of experience.

However, the advent of the digital era has led to, on one hand, the ability to gather more than simple aggregate statistics, at a very low cost but with potentially significant benefits (for example, consider the possibility of detailed reports on the performance of individual hospitals, in real time, based on data that hospitals gather anyway). On the other hand, digitization can also make it easier to *conceal* information. For instance, this is true for the diffusion of news. While newspapers have always been public, and the same can be said for mass gatherings, instead the diffusion of a fabricated news story inside certain WhatsApp groups will only be observed by members of those groups, and, as emphasized by Carole Cadwalladr's TED talk,[6] misleading election ads on Facebook leave no trace (outside of Facebook's own servers, which are inaccessible to the public). Similarly, until a few years ago, financial trading was primarily done by physical traders in large, crowded rooms, which have been almost completely replaced by quiet, private offices filled with screens.

Evidence–based policy making in the new millennium does not simply entail that censuses are run more efficiently or more often. It must also entail establishing which information flows *already taking place* in our markets and societies are worth monitoring and studying because of their systemic significance. And this is not done by requiring more paperwork from individual citizens, but rather by requiring compliance from private companies and infrastructures that handle such data.

Finally, although the anonymity of nodes is not always foolproof, reminding that network analysis *does not need names or other individual identification* can still help quell Orwellian feelings of absolute control. If we recall the discussion of important network, edge, and node characteristics from Chapter 1, node *names* or *labels* are, in fact, irrelevant to understanding whether or not a network is prone to contagion. If somehow a node *does* assume a systemically significant role, and hence requires special interventions or monitoring — as in the case of a large bank or a systematic distributor of fabricated news — then its anonymity will presumably become a secondary concern.

6.3 Dynamic regulation

In the aftermath of the 2008 Lehman Brothers bankruptcy and of the collapse that followed it, central banks all around the world, including the Federal Reserve, reacted with measures aimed at stimulating the economy — first and foremost lowering short–term interest rates in order to provide funding where banks were retreating. Central bankers and governments knew they had to reassure market players *as soon as possible*, because otherwise the crisis would only worsen with every minute that passed.

But what if short–term interest rates had been *automatically* linked to indicators of market turmoil, such as reduced connectedness of financial networks? Not only would such measures have taken place immediately, but market players would have also *known* in advance that, even in the event of troubles for certain big banks, policy measures were in place to prevent the credit crunch from spreading to the real economy. This could have limited the escalation of panic.

A dynamic, reactive, network–aware regulation could go even further than that by acting at the *node* level. The Basel III accords dictate general requirements and yearly stress tests for banks, but the real–time analysis of centrality indicators for each bank (made possible by data and tools available today to central banks and bodies such as the ESRP) could allow regulators to automatically trigger specific measures, or checks, for specific banks, based on their likelihood of being hit by, or triggering, cascades of financial distress. Again, knowing that regulations include automatic countercyclical stabilizers would increase market participants' trust in the system, and in their peers.

Moreover, detection rules based on network measures can be more accurate instruments to reach desired stability targets. Imposing Basel III capital requirements on banks is a bit like ordering each citizen to take an aspirin every day: it certainly helps prevent heart attacks, but it is not free of side effects, nor is it a *guarantee* against heart attacks. If the risk of heart attack in the population is high, aspirin might be better than nothing, but 24/7 heart monitoring devices that constantly transmit data to specialists in real time would certainly be preferred. And it should be clear by now that the kind of data specialists need to evaluate the risk of financial distress is not limited to a few numbers from a given bank's balance sheet; rather, such analysis involves the position of the bank itself within the network of financial relations — that is, the actual financial relations.

In general, disclosure requirements and dynamic regulation provide an interesting 'third way' in the eternal debate about the role of the state in the economy. If we wanted to simplify this debate in just one sentence, we could say that the 'left' view promotes a state which must regulate otherwise unjust, inefficient, and even self–destructive markets, while the 'right' view considers markets mostly self–regulating, public interventions as distorting the natural functioning of the economy, and 'laissez–faire' (French for 'let do') as the ideal state approach to private transactions.

Collecting high quality data that allows us to better understand important socioeconomic phenomena (such as the spread of fake news or the role of derivatives in financial markets), enabling authorized research groups to analyze that data, creating tools that track the behavior of a system in real time, and choosing regulations and stabilizers that automatically respond to the first symptoms of distress, represents a new approach to policymaking (although one that does not exclude more traditional prudential requirements, such as leverage caps). This observation certainly does not 'solve' the left–right debate, but it does provide a clear policy direction which both visions *must* accept, because collecting information is increasingly useful, increasingly cheap, and does not result in the 'market distortions' of which state interventions in the economy are sometimes accused. This is even more true when information is *already owned* by single market participants.

There are, and always have been, good arguments both for why the state should intervene in the economy and for why it should not; the optimal degree of intervention is a tradeoff between these two viewpoints and also depends on a particular country's cultural values and historical traits. However, in a world that is rapidly changing, regulation must keep pace. Information is the real resource of the twenty–first century, and given the profound impact data analysis has had on many sectors, the fact that it still has not taken an *organic* place in how regulation is implemented is worrisome.

Giants like Amazon and Facebook, but also millions of smaller companies worldwide, do not examine their customer's data once in a while to produce reports on past activity and make new plans accordingly. In the business world, data is an organic component of production systems, exploited in order to make recommendations for new products, determine the prices of plane tickets, guide research for new product features, display targeted ads on web pages, and make special offers to gain customers' loyalty. So why should financial constraints for banks consist of mere thresholds, set in stone once every few years, and even then typically when it is too late — that is, after a financial downturn?

Compared to the extent to which corporations and capital flows transcend national borders, the level of cooperation and harmonization between regulatory agencies around the world is quite minimal. The need for the international alignment of policies should not be interpreted as a forced assimilation to regulations from one country to others or as the abolition of trade barriers. Rather, regulation must keep pace with the extent to which barriers between national societies and economies are removed, regulation must keep the pace. Like the debate between right–wing and left–wing economists, the pros and cons of globalization could fill entire books. But the important point is that, to the extent to which economic and social networks become global, their regulation must also be made global.

6.4 Coordinated growth

From the individual point of view, stating that our world is becoming *more interconnected* does not amount to merely recognizing the increase of physical and virtual devices connecting individuals, firms and institutions around the world — be they cable or Wi-Fi connections, mobile phone microwaves, or satellite communications. Rather it means acknowledging that our *actions* and *daily routines* are increasingly interdependent with those of other people. Actions as simple as pushing a 'share' or 'like' button can impact other people's well–being, on the other side of the street, or on the other side of the planet.

In the previous chapter, we have learned that nodes in financial networks tend to synchronize their behavior, and that this can represent an additional source of risk for the stability of the financial system. And just like in the case of the Millennium Bridge, whose wobbling derived from the fact that the steps of the crowd would spontaneously coordinate, synchronization of market participants can be spontaneous, and sometimes even undetected by market participants. This natural propensity to behave similarly is important not just for phenomena occurring on social and economic networks, but for the *structure* itself of networks, because it shapes their growth.

For instance, at the end of Chapter 2 we have seen that many networks feature an extreme heterogeneity in the degree of nodes, similar to the scale–free 'synthetic' networks that can be produced with the preferential attachment model, where new nodes tend to attach to the most connected among the already existing nodes. But this is not a coincidence: the fact is that virtually all social or economic networks grow according to *some form* of preferential attachment that establishes what edges will be formed. In social and economic networks, nobody builds edges randomly. Every time a friendship is formed (or recorded within an online social network), every time a financial transaction is established, every time a road or a railway is built connecting two places, such action is directed by the perspective of some benefit. In some cases, these benefits are

Figure 6.3 Panel located at the boundary between the drainage basins of Danube and Rhein

quite *idiosyncratic* in nature — I befriend someone because there is just something *I* like about that person, something making me think that I will enjoy her company (and vice–versa): something that other people may not like as much. But in other cases, different nodes will have similar motives pushing them to build connections. Already in the case of friendship, it is obvious that there are people that are just *better* than others at making (and keeping) friends — maybe they are *objectively* more funny, or cheerful? But in other networks, the motives of different actors for forming network edges are aligned almost by definition. At least in principle, financial institutions all look for *the same thing* when allowing a credit line to another institution: an affordable debtor that will reliably repay a debt — possibly with a high premium.

Within a small forest in the territory of Wilhelmsdorf, a German town in the Bavaria region, one can find the panel depicted in Figure 6.3. It signals the border between the drainage basins of the Rhine and the Danube, the two longest rivers in Central and Western Europe. What this means is that a drop of rain falling on the left side of the panel will, after a journey of more than one thousand kilometers, flow into the Northern Sea, while one falling on the right will, after an even longer journey, flow into the Black Sea, on the opposite side of Europe. These two drops are guided by the same exact physical force — gravity — and will ultimately both end up in the same huge patch of water formed by our planet's seas and oceans, but while doing so, they will take completely different routes along the network formed by the two rivers and their affluents. The drops' 'aim' is not to reach any specific sea: they just move downward, and whatever path guiding them downwards will work.

In the same way, financial institutions vary under many dimensions, including their geographic location and level of risk of their investments, but despite this, their actions are driven by very similar forces. Which does not necessarily mean that they will form edges connecting them to the same nodes — say, lend money to a specific firm, or sector, that shows promising prospects. It means however that *even if they happen to connect to nodes that could seem remote between them*, they do it pushed by a similar motive: an economic force that carves routes — sometimes long and crooked — connecting capitals to (hopefully) profitable investments. So the example, featured in Figure 5.2 of the previous chapter, of two banks B and C that provide credit to the same shipbuilding companies (unbeknownst to their common creditor Bank A — and possibly to each other) is not just a curious coincidence, but a foreseeable consequence of those companies arguably representing a good investment — to the eyes of both banks.

Financial networks are only one of the many instances where a node's reason to connect to a given other node goes way *beyond* the characteristics of that other node. If the inhabitants of an isolated town in a remote region want to plan a road connecting them to their country's road network, they will be scarcely interested in the amenities offered by the specific location where the new road will join an old one. The new road's goal is not to reach the intersection: it is to reach the entire network. Similarly, users of an online social network might want to connect with — for instance to follow, on X — users who tend to propose the most interesting, or funniest, or most beautiful content; but the content these users propose is more often forwarded (for example, retweeted) than created out of the blue, which implies that they serve as a *gateway* to information provided by the rest of the network.

All of this is reflected in the shape that networks ultimately take. It has a strong impact on their propensity to propagate contagion, which is just the 'dark side' of connectedness — connectedness typically being something that networks spontaneously 'aim' for. Ultimately, the structure of many human networks is not just *susceptible* to contagion: their complex and long-lasting growth process has made them *optimized* for contagion. And just as water flows around obstacles, new connections will tend to spontaneously — or even strategically, in some cases — replace any blocked ones, as in the case of travelers from China to Italy at the beginning of the pandemic.

This does not mean that contagion cannot be stopped: appropriate policies can be deployed if, as discussed previously in this chapter, the networked nature of a phenomenon is understood and tamed. It does mean, however, that the best way to tackle issues related to contagion includes an attention to how networks *grow* over time, and hence to the motives that push network members to build connections. Not just policymakers, but also individual nodes can be helped in understanding the risks they bear and procure by being part of a network, and of how to best protect from them.

6.5 *An inescapable network of mutuality*

Social networks bridge gaps not just across geographic distances, but also across social distances. Until quite recently, in Western countries. the distinction between politicians, businessmen, and journalists (and previously, aristocrats), on one side, and 'ordinary people', on the other side, was relatively clear, in terms of their ability to influence public opinion. Today this distinction is more blurred, with 'influencers' emerging on social media platforms without any specific career path, credentialing, or achievement. Similarly, the decrease in transport costs means that more people can travel across the world, and even barriers to financial markets have been lowered, with several commercial banks offering their customers the ability to become traders in their free time. This larger dynamism gives rise to many opportunities, but it also makes the systems more complex and responsibilities more diffused.

As human beings, we are simply not used to such complex environments. Our systems of values, our laws, and even our mental abilities took thousands of years to adapt to the small societies — typically villages — of our remote ancestors. Urbanization was a major social change (still ongoing) not just because it introduced new professions and increased economic interaction — urban residents typically do not produce the food they eat — but also because it completely changed our social landscape. Living in a city means meeting, interacting with, and maybe discussing issues with people we do not know, or at least recognize, every day. Our mental abilities have not had time to adapt (research shows that we recognize an average of five thousand faces,[7] which is enough to easily cover the inhabitants of a village, but certainly not of a metropolis), but several of our laws and habits have.

Moving social and economic interactions to the online sphere — or onto other kinds of global networks — represents a further, even more drastic change. For instance, people we meet on X are 'different' from people we meet on the bus because we might not even see their face. The sheer number of participants in online debates makes it even more difficult to attribute them personal traits, a reputation, or some level of trust — all elements that play a crucial role in the way we form our opinions. Similarly, economic transactions are concluded increasingly often between ordinary citizens who ignore each other's identity and disregard whether they will ever meet again. This new transition is happening now, and is changing society at an even faster pace than urbanization did.

Maybe digital natives will develop not only technical, but also social skills that allow them to exercise the required judgment when receiving news that lacks appropriate sources through online social networks. It is possible they will spontaneously attempt to track their origin, looking for trusted nodes along their diffusion path. Maybe spreading fake news, even inadvertently, will become a significant source of social shame. After all, new technologies make it so easy to fabricate 'credible' evidence — as in the phenomenon of deepfakes, the do–it–yourself fabricated videos that are hardly distinguishable as such[8] and are made so easy by the progress of artificial intelligence — that reconstructing the source becomes the *only* criterion for credibility (although chatbots such as ChatGPT tend to go in the opposite direction of hiding and concealing the sources). Or maybe social networks as a whole will suffer from a credibility crisis, and people will again search for a few, well-known, authoritative newspaper news sources, keeping X, Facebook, TikTok, and their successors solely for sharing pictures of kittens, or new hit songs. Maybe parents will caution their children not to 'take news from strangers' (and chatbots) much like they caution against taking candy from strangers today.

And maybe, this change of approach to social networks will not 'just' be motivated by the self–serving desire to discriminate true information from fabricated news, to benefit from the use of a new technology, or to avoid online frauds. Future generations will change their approach because they will find it *self–evident* that every action made within a social network, be it a retweet or a vaccine shot, has repercussions across the entire social network itself; repercussions that may affect people we will never know, but that it would still be unethical to ignore.

Just like the Eiffel Tower, transmission towers are usually composed of multiple independent sections of metal joined together, rather than a single monolithic block of metal. This does not make them *fragile*, but it does imply that each single piece of metal is in some way responsible for the stability and robustness of the entire structure — just like in complex, and strongly interconnected, modern societies.

Notes

1 Interestingly, some recent legal theories about attribution of responsibility (Engl, 2022) implicitly define responsibility as *proximity*, on a network of 'states of the world', to the actual implementation of an action.
2 http://nytimes.com/2008/10/31/business/worldbusiness/31norris.html
3 Battiston, 2016.
4 https://nytimes.com/interactive/2019/12/19/opinion/location-tracking-cell-phone.html
5 https://techcrunch.com/2006/08/06/aol-proudly-releases-massive-amounts-of-user-search-data
6 Carole Cadwalladr, TED2019, April 15, 2019, https://ted.com/talks/carole_cadwalladr_facebook_s_role_in_brexit_and_the_threat_to_democracy
7 Jenkins, Dowsett, and Burton, 2018.
8 https://nytimes.com/2018/03/04/technology/fake-videos-deepfakes.html

Bibliography

Battiston, Pietro (2016). 'Constrained Network Formation'. In: *Italian Economic Journal* 2.3, pp. 347–362.

Engl, Florian (2022). 'A Theory of Causal Responsibility Attribution'. In: *CESifo Working Papers, Nr. 9898*.

Jenkins, R, AJ Dowsett, and AM Burton (2018). 'How many faces do people know?' In: *Proceedings of the Royal Society B* 285.1888, p. 20181319.

Vitali, Stefania, James B Glattfelder, and Stefano Battiston (2011). 'The Network of Global Corporate Control'. In: *PloS One* 6.10, p. e25995.

Image credits

Where not otherwise stated, figures are the author's own work.

- 1.1a: CC-Attribution, Eghdam et al., 2018
- 1.1b: CC-Attribution, Chamberlain et al., 2018
- 1.1c: CC-Attribution, Jacoby, Papastamatiou, and Freeman, 2016
- 1.1h: CC-Attribution, Guleva et al., 2017
- 1.1i: CC-Attribution, Li et al., 2017
- 1.1j: Public Domain, https://commons.wikimedia.org/wiki/File:Reseau_autoroutier_francais.svg, user *madcap*
- 1.1k: CC-Attribution, Gallos et al., 2013
- 1.1l: CC-Attribution, Choi et al., 2017
- 1.1m: CC-Attribution, Fajardo-Ortiz et al., 2017
- 1.1n: CC-Attribution, https://commons.wikimedia.org/wiki/File:Internet_map_1024_-_transparent,_inverted.png, users *Rezonansowy* and *Matt Britt*
- 1.1o: CC0 Universal Public Domain Dedication, https://commons.wikimedia.org/wiki/File:DNA_chemical_structure.svg, by Madeleine Price Ball
- 1.1p: CC-Attribution, Catalá-López et al., 2012
- 1.9: Open Database License, ©OpenStreetMap contributors
- 3.1: Open Database License, ©OpenStreetMap contributors
- 3.5: Public Domain, CDC, MMWR Morb Mortal Wkly Rep, 2021
- 3.7: CC-Attribution, Mossong et al., 2008
- 3.9: CC-Attribution, Melegaro et al., 2017
- 6.3 GFDL license, https://commons.wikimedia.org/wiki/File:D-BW-Wilhelmsdorf_-_Pfrunger-Burgweiler_Ried_-_Europäische_Wasserscheide.JPG, user *ANKAWÜ*

Bibliography

Catalá-López, Ferrán et al. (2012). 'Coauthorship and institutional collaborations on cost-effectiveness analyses: a systematic network analysis'. In: *PLoS One* 7.5, p. e38012.

CDC, MMWR Morb Mortal Wkly Rep (2021). 'COVID-19 Stats: COVID-19 Incidence, by Age Group — United States, March 1–November 14'. Tech. rep. URL: https://cdc.gov/mmwr/volumes/69/wr/mm695152a8.htm

Chamberlain, Benjamin Paul et al. (2018). 'Real-time community detection in full social networks on a laptop'. In: *PloS One* 13.1, p. e0188702.

Choi, Jaesuk et al. (2017). 'A novel smart navigation system for intramedullary nailing in orthopedic surgery'. In: *PloS One* 12.4, p. e0174407.

Eghdam, Aboozar et al. (2018). 'Facebook as communication support for persons with potential mild acquired cognitive impairment: A content and social network analysis study'. In: *PloS One* 13.1, p. e0191878.

Fajardo-Ortiz, David et al. (2017). 'The emergence and evolution of the research fronts in HIV/AIDS research'. In: *PloS One* 12.5, p. e0178293.

Gallos, Lazaros K et al. (2013). 'IMDB network revisited: unveiling fractal and modular properties from a typical small-world network'. In: *PloS One* 8.6, p. e66443.

Guleva, Valentina Y. et al. (2017). 'A Simulation Tool for Exploring the Evolution of Temporal Interbank Networks'. In: *Journal of Artificial Societies and Social Simulation* 20.4, p. 15. ISSN: 1460-7425.

Jacoby, David MP, Yannis P Papastamatiou, and Robin Freeman (2016). 'Inferring animal social networks and leadership: applications for passive monitoring arrays'. In: *Journal of the Royal Society Interface* 13.124, p. 20160676.

Li, Fangzhou et al. (2017). 'Measuring directional urban spatial interaction in China: A migration perspective'. In: *PloS One* 12.1, p. e0171107.

Melegaro, Alessia et al. (2017). 'Social contact structures and time use patterns in the Manicaland Province of Zimbabwe'. In: *PloS One* 12.1, p. e0170459.

Mossong, Joël et al. (2008). 'Social contacts and mixing patterns relevant to the spread of infectious diseases'. In: *PLoS Medicine* 5.3, p. e74.

Index

Abrams, Jenna 77–79
adversarial node removal 33, 35
antitrust 120–122
asset 96
assortativity 17, 30–31, 90, 93–84, 97

Banco Popular 110–111
BBC Pandemic 60
bank run 92, 111
Basel Committee for Banking Supervision 107
Basel III accords 108, 113, 120, 126
basic reproduction number *see* number

Cambridge Analytica 87, 125
cascade 70–73, 77
Central CounterPart 114–115
CCP *see* Central CounterPart
CDO see Collateralized Debt Obligation
CDS *see* Credit Default Swap
centrality 17–19, 31, 36, 83, 85, 119, 126; betweenness 19; eigenvector 19; Katz 19; PageRank 18
ChatGPT 79, 131
clearing 114
closeness 18
clustering 15–16
Coase theorem 25
CoCo bond *see* COntingent COnvertible bond
Collateralized Debt Obligation 106–107, 114–117
compartment 48
compartmental model *see* compartment
complex system 36–37
component 32; giant 32
compression 112–113
contagion 28–29, 31, 37, 119–120, 130; epidemiologic 39–52; financial 97–98, 111; informational 68–72
coauthorship 45
COntingent COnvertible bond 111
contact tracing app 59–60
coordination 92, 103
COVID–19 39–40, 42–44, 47–50, 52–54, 58–62, 65–76, 123
Credit Default Swap 102
cycle *see* loop

DAG *see* graph
debt 102
degree 10–13, 16–17, 28–30, 34–36, 45–47, 82–83, 95–96, 113, 128; average 13, 29, 45, 50; six degrees hypothesis 21; weighted 11
density 13–15, 33, 47
derivative 102–103, 113–114, 121, 124
diameter 14, 19–20, 34–35, 44
disassortativity *see* assortativity
distance 12, 96, 106, 110, 115; average 13–14, 19–22, 28–29, 44, 59

Ebola 40–45, 48–50, 53, 55, 61, 70, 74, 120
edge 2
equity 102
Erdős, Paul 20–21
Erdős: number *see* number; –Rényi model 34–35
ESRB *see* European Systemic Risk Board
Exposure Notification protocol 60
European Systemic Risk Board 124
expectations 98
exponential growth 47–49, 67, 77
externality 26–28, 87, 93, 107

Facebook 2–5, 15–17, 21–22, 29, 59
fact checking 86
fake news 74–76, 84–87, 120, 131
filter bubble 84

fractional reserve 94; banking 94–95, 97, 113
flu *see* influenza
FluPhone 60
follower 4, 6–8, 10–13, 69–73, 79–87, 119–120; ghost 78
fungus 4
fungibility 96

Galton's ox 81
Gangnam Style 67–68, 70
giant component 32
global: measure 12–14; global value chain 90
graph: Directed Acyclic 70; theory 20

herd immunity 50
HIT *see* herd immunity
HIV 45, 74
hop 11
homophily *see* assortativity
Horner, Paul 84–85
hub 34

IMM *see* Internal Model Method
incubation time 47, 68, 71
indegree *see* degree
influencer 89, 131
influenza 60; avian 71
Internal Model Method 109
International Securities Identification Numbers 124
Internet Research Agency 78
ISIN *see* International Securities Identification Numbers

Joint Supervisory Team 109–110
JST *see* Joint Supervisory Team

Legal Entity Identifier 124
Lehman Brothers 91
LEI *see* Legal Entity Identifier
leverage 94, 113, 115; cap 127
Lewandowski, Corey 84
liability 93–94, 106
link *see* edge
local measure 12, 31
logarithmic scale 49, 67
look–through 110
loop 16; 111–112

MacIntyre, C. Raina 40
matrix: social contact 54–59; WAIFW 73
Matthew effect 34
maturity structure 93
measles 50, 53, 58, 74
meme 67, 73
money: central bank 94; commercial bank 94–95, 113
moral hazard 109
Musk, Elon 79

natural language processing 72–73
network 2; archipelago 16; circle 16; complete 16; directed 5, 10–11, 13–14, 19; effect 27; ego 28, 97, 100; Erdős–Rényi *see* Erdős; growth 9, 34–35; multiplex 72, 102–103; resilient 33–35; scale–free 35, 44, 128; social 70–73; spatial 9, 90; star 16, 33–34, 76; theory 27; weighted 6, 8, 11, 19, 51, 95
NLP *see* natural language processing
node 2
novation 114
number: basic reproduction 49; Erdős 20–21; Kevin Bacon 21

Obama, Barack 7
OTC *see* over–the–counter trading
outdegree *see* degree
over–the–counter trading 114

PageRank 18, 86; *see also* centrality
Panama Papers 115
patient zero 45
path 11–13, 96, 110, 122–123; circular *see* loop; shortest 18, 20–22
People You May Know 83–84
persuasion bias 82
pollution 25–27
preferential attachment 34
privacy 60, 124
protectionism 123
public interest (X account) 87

R_0 *see* basic reproduction number
resilience 33–35
rewiring 30
Risk Weighted Assets 108
RWA see Risk Weighted Assets

securitization 105, 106
shadow banking 115
small world 20, 22, 31, 44; Columbia project 20
social distancing 67
Special Purpose Vehicle 105
spread 99
SPV *see* Special Purpose Vehicle

SREP *see* Supervisory Review and Evaluation Process
star: network *see* network; node 35, 44
stock market 91
stress test 110, 113
superspreader 44
superspreading event 44
Supervisory Review and Evaluation Process 109, 117
systemic: importance 35, 95, 102, 114, 126; risk 114, 124

topology 34–35, 104
Trending Topics (Facebook) 85
TriOptima 113–114
Trump, Donald 7, 78, 84–85, 123
Trump, Eric 84
Twitter *see* X

US: highway system 31; presidential elections 78

Vespignani, Alessandro 62
Viral content 67–71
Virus (computer) 9

WAIFW *see* matrix
wisdom of the crowds 81

X 4–8, 77–79

Kolibri 360 GmbH
Ferdinand-Jühlke-Straße 7
99095 Erfurt, Deutschland
produktsicherheit@kolibri360.de